Come On! Rewrite The Australian Constitution

by Jill Archer

CONTENTS

Foreword   i

1. The Need for a New Constitution   1

2. The Queen   3

3. The Governor-General   10

4. The People   25

5. The House of Representatives   34

6. The Senate   55

7. Where the Parliament Can Decide   62

8. Prescribed Parliamentary Powers   71

9. A Referendum is Required   78

10. The States   86

11. The Territories   102

12. The Judicature   104

13. Redundant Sections of the Constitution   107

14. Altering the Current Constitution   109

15. Creating a New Constitution   111

16. An Updated Australian Constitution   114

Foreword

It is likely that Australia will have a Commonwealth Labor government in 2019. This party proposes to hold a referendum on whether Australia should become a republic by asking, as a first step, for a simple 'Yes' or "No' from voters. Australia has been down this road before. A referendum in 1999 proposed a law to:

'alter the Constitution to establish the Commonwealth of Australia as a Republic with the Queen and Governor-General being replaced by a President appointed by a two-thirds majority of the members of the Commonwealth Parliament'. The referendum was lost.

Any move to a republic must include a review of the present Constitution. Tinkering with the text to replace the Queen and Governor-General with a President could have significant implications for the role of a new head-of-state and be a lost opportunity to reassess our Federation.

There will be familiar arguments as to why Australia should remain a Constitutional Monarchy. We have just had a visit from the Duke and Duchess of Sussex which some say will put paid to any thought of Australia becoming a republic. However, most countries in the Commonwealth of Nations are Republics.

The Duke and Duchess of Cambridge toured the Republics of Singapore and India in 2012 and 2016 respectively. Harry and Meghan called in on the Republic of Fiji this year. These countries are members of the Commonwealth of Nations. The Republic of Australia will still be received into the Commonwealth of Nations and can be on the royal visitor list.

It will be alleged that our present system is not broken so why change it. Australians have spent much of Federation thinking about changing the Constitution with very little to show for all the Committees and Conventions. There was; a Royal Commission on the Constitution (1927-29), a Joint Parliamentary Committee on Constitutional Review (1956-59), an Australian Constitutional Convention (1973-1985), a Constitutional Commission (1988), a 1991 Centenary Conference with a Constitutional Centenary Foundation to educate Australian about the Constitution and a Constitutional Convention (1998). Someone, somewhere must have felt the need for an update.

Australia is a different place to what it was in 1901. The States were envisioned as the dominate partner in Federation and to be financially independent. Over time, the Commonwealth has assumed more power due to a broad reading of the Constitution by the High Court and after the Second World War, took over the income tax system from the States. This means the States must rely on revenue from the Goods and Services Tax (GST), Commonwealth Grants (which can be tied to specific purposes) and local revenue streams from gambling and stamp duties. Australians find it hard to know which tier of government is responsible for services and how funding is achieved, or how our system of government works (much of which does not rate a mention in the Constitution). Few would want to read the Constitution in its present form. It is riddled with redundancy as sections have ceased to be relevant and is highly legalistic making it difficult to comprehend. Voters do not feel ownership of their Constitution and need reform which gives control where it belongs. It is well known that people are more satisfied with their situation if they feel they have more control. Public confidence in Commonwealth Governments in recent years is at a low ebb. A citizen-led rewrite of the Constitution is a chance for people to put their stamp on how they want Australia to be governed.

Current politicians are never likely to do more than a minimalist change to our Constitution and then only in an ad hoc way that may or may not receive the endorsement of voters. If difficult issues arise such as same-sex marriage or euthanasia, politicians hide behind conscience votes (what ever they are) that may not reflect the wishes of their electorate. Tony Abbott campaigned for the 'No' vote in the same-sex marriage survey whilst seventy five percent of his electorate of

Warringah voted 'Yes'. Abbott then went on to abstain during the Parliamentary vote. Taberner and Zorzetto (A Short History of Climate Change Policy in Australia, 2014) outline the process the Federal Government has gone through from 1992 until 2014 in an attempt to legislate a mechanism to price carbon emissions. The major political parties cooperated on policy initially only to see legislation abandoned due to adversarial politics. Could a more reasoned examination of the Henry Taxation review in 2009 have properly funded the Gonski education reforms and the National Disability Insurance Scheme? The Constitution says nothing about evidence-based policy development and the ability to explain policy to the electorate. Perhaps it should.

This book attempts to summarise the present Constitution and points out some of the changes made to our system of Federation to try and work around an archaic document. It then presents a possible revamp, in plain English and some ways in which Australian citizens can take back control of the Commonwealth by rewriting their law.

1. The Need for a New Constitution

The Australian Constitution was drafted in the 1890's when Australia was part of the British Empire. It was designed to bring six colonies (Western Australia, South Australia, Queensland, New South Wales, Victoria and Tasmania) into a new Federation based around financial, trade and defence issues. The Constitution was developed during two Conventions, principally by men with important positions in the Colony. The draft was take to England where it was enacted by the British Parliament as the Commonwealth of Australia Constitution Act, 1900. Section 9 of this Act contains the text of the Australian Constitution.

I have tried to read the Constitution but found it a difficult exercise. It has some redundancy as sections concerned with a transition to Federation have ceased to be relevant, it seems unnecessarily wordy, terms and phrases are not defined, the Commonwealth Government has been given licence to make the rules where the Constitution allows and the text is hard to comprehend. For example:

Section 97 Audit: Until the Parliament otherwise provides, the laws in force in any Colony which has become or becomes a State with respect to the receipt of revenue and the expenditure of money on account of the Government of the Colony, and the review and audit of such receipt and expenditure, shall apply to the receipt of revenue and the expenditure of money on account of the Commonwealth in the State in the same manner as if the Commonwealth, or the Government or an officer of the Commonwealth, were mentioned whenever the Colony, or the Government or an officer of the Colony, is mentioned. Furthermore, it doesn't seem to bear much resemblance to how the current Commonwealth Government works. Could members of the Commonwealth Parliament put their hand on the present Constitution and swear to serve the people of Australia?

There have been numerous attempts to alter the Constitution by means of referendums, Commissions, Conferences, Conventions and Committees. So much time and money and little to show for it. This is my attempt to condense the Constitution so I can begin to understand it. To try and reconcile this document with what is currently the practice of the Commonwealth Government and indicate ramifications of altering the Constitution to accommodate a Republic. If my interpretations are wrong and some are bound to be, that may tell something about the Australian Constitution. It is supposed to be the people's document, grasped by all.

2. The Queen

Given Australia was a British Colony when the Constitution was enacted, it is expected the British Monarch would have a role in the government of Australia and the present Constitution bears this out. The Queen's powers (exercised by the Governor-General) are left over from times when the sovereign had more authority. These powers are now largely undertaken by the Federal Government. According to the Australian Constitution this is where the Queen is mentioned.

1. The Parliament of the Commonwealth consists of the Queen, a Senate, and a House of Representatives. Section 1.
2. The Queen appoints a Governor-General to be her representative in the Commonwealth and this person is assigned functions by the Queen (in keeping with the Constitution). Section 2.
3. The Queen receives monies from the Consolidated Revenue fund of the Commonwealth so she can pay the Governor-General an annual sum of ten thousand pounds (which the Parliament can vary). Section 3.
4. The Queen can appoint persons other than the Governor-General to administer the Government of the Commonwealth. Section 4.

5. One of the qualifications of a member of the Commonwealth Parliament is that he (all persons in the Constitution are 'he') is a subject of the Queen (natural born or naturalised for at least five years under the law of the United Kingdom, a State of Australia or the Commonwealth). The Parliament can otherwise provide. Section 34.

6. A member of Parliament cannot receive monies from the Crown or the Commonwealth over and above entitlements as a member. That is, unless he is one of the Queen's Ministers of State or in the Queen's or the Commonwealth's army or navy. Section 44 (iv).

7. The Governor-General assents, or otherwise, to laws passed in the Commonwealth Parliament in the Queen's name. The Governor-General may reserve a law for the Queen's pleasure and she has two years to decide on assent or otherwise. Sections 58 and 60.

8. The Queen may disallow any law up to one year after the Governor-General has given assent. Section 59.

9. The Queen, through the Governor-General, has the power to execute the laws of the Commonwealth. Section 61.

10. Members of Parliament who become Ministers are known as the Queen's Ministers of State and the salaries of these Ministers are paid by the Queen out of the Consolidated Revenue Fund of the Commonwealth. The Parliament can otherwise provide. Sections 64 and 66.

11. Appeals can be made to the High Court for referral to the Queen in Council, otherwise known as the Privy Council (appeals from Australian Courts were abolished in 1986). Sections 73 and 74

12. A Queen's subject in one State is to be treated equally in another State. Section 117.

13. The Queen may place a Territory under the authority of the Commonwealth which can grant this Territory Parliamentary representation. Section 122.

14. The Queen can authorise the Governor-General to appoint any person(s) to be his deputy throughout the Commonwealth and can have a say in this person's powers and functions. Section 126.

Comments: The Queen is at the heart of the Commonwealth Parliament but what does she really do?

Instructions to the Governor-General:

- At Federation, in 1900, Queen Victoria signed a number of documents relating to the future Commonwealth of Australia. One of these established the office of the Governor-General and a document, The Letters Patent, gave instructions to the Governor-General on how to perform his constitutional duties.

- In 1984, Queen Elizabeth, on the advice of Prime Minister Hawke, revoked Queen Victoria's Letters Patent and

Instructions to the Governor-General and issued new documents clarifying the Governor-General's position. This consisted of detailing how any deputy or administrator (as per section 4 of the Constitution) would be appointed if the Governor-General was out of the country or unable to do his duties (along with the publication of any such arrangements). The new Letters Patent also specified that the incoming Governor-General (or an appointed administrator) would take, in the presence of a High Court judge, an oath or affirmation or allegiance to the Queen and an oath or affirmation of Office (to the Commonwealth of Australia).

- The latest Letters Patent 2008, reinforce Section 4 of the Constitution regarding a stand-in for the Governor-General and the fact that this substitute must act on the advice of the Governor-General, the Prime Minister or a Minister of State. The two oaths of allegiance to the Queen and The Commonwealth must also be taken by this person. In the new Letters Patent it may seem as if the Governor-General's powers have been reduced to nominating a stand-in. However, with so few instructions from the Queen, does this give the Governor-General more independence in the role or less?

<u>The Queen's exercise of powers when in Australia:</u>

- Instruction to the Governor-General from the Queen would now be on the advice of the Commonwealth Government. They were probably always irrelevant, as even though Queen Victoria established the Office of the Governor-General, the Constitution outlines the powers and responsibilities of this person. Furthermore, there is some doubt over whether the Queen can direct the Governor-General. In 1953, for the 1954 royal visit, Prime Minister Menzies brought on the 'Royal Powers Act, (1953)' which gave the Queen, while in Australia, the ability to exercise any power under the Constitution which was exercisable by the Governor-General. The need for this Act indicates that all powers reside with the Governor-General (except the power to appoint himself which belongs to the Queen on the advice of the Prime Minister).

<u>Payment of the Governor-General and Government Ministers by the Queen:</u>

- The Governor-General's salary is set for incoming Governors by the Parliament under the 'Governor-General Act 1974'. By convention, this salary is similar to that received by the Chief Justice of the High Court. On retirement, Governor-Generals receive a non-contributory pension for life which, like their salary, may be set to take account of pension entitlements from previous employment.

- The Renumeration Tribunal is an independent statutory body that handles the payment of key Commonwealth Officers such as Federal Parliamentarians, Federal Judges and Departmental Heads.
- Any role by the Queen is effectively extinguished.

Queen of Australia

- Elizabeth the Second is not only Queen of the United Kingdom but also Queen of Australia. In 1953 and 1973 under 'The Royal Style and Titles Acts', Queen Elizabeth was titled Elizabeth the Second, by the Grace of God Queen of Australia and Her other Realms and Territories, Head of the Commonwealth. A Queen of Australia who is also head of the Anglican Church is somewhat anachronistic in a modern multicultural Australia.

Some will say it doesn't matter what the Constitution says about the Queen or her successors. In practice the sovereign does little except visit occasionally. However, if a constitution is meant to contain the guiding principles on the way a country is governed, why not remove the historical references (or consign them to a Preamble) and update the document. Why does the Constitution need the Queen? If her powers are exercisable only while in Australia and she can only appoint the Governor-General on the advice of the Government, in reality she retains only a ceremonial role. However, there is the outside possibility that a British monarch could exercise constitutional power in Australia by being physically present. News of the Royal Family will always be available in print and online media and they can visit at any time (although not necessarily at Australia's expense). Australia will still be welcome in the Commonwealth of Nations. Republics such as India, South Africa, Singapore and Pakistan are among the fifty three republics in this body.

Australia, in the twenty first century, does not need a British sovereign woven into its Constitution.

3. The Governor-General

Historically, Britain relied on governors, appointed by the Monarch, on the advice of the British Government, to administer colonies. The early Governor-Generals were usually from the British aristocracy and represented Britain's interests in the Empire. The Governor-General was a channel of communication between the Australian and British Governments to keep the British informed about Australian government business and other matters. In 1926, an Imperial Conference resulted in the 1931, 'Statute of Westminster'. This set out, as law, the independence of the Dominions (Australia, New Zealand, Canada and Eire). Britain could only enact laws concerning the Dominions at the government of a Dominion's request. One result of the Statute was the appointment, in 1930, of Sir Isaac Isaacs, Australia's Chief Justice at the time, to be the first Governor-General recommended by an Australian Prime Minister.

Australia adopted the above Statute in 1942, as 'The Statute of Westminster Adoption Act'. This Act, along with the 1986 'Australia Act', removed all possibility that the British Parliament could be involved in the Federal Government of Australia or the States and Territories. The Australia Act largely removed a role for the Queen in the Constitution and also effectively removed an appeal by an Australian court to the British Privy Council.

The Australian Constitution, put together in the late eighteen hundreds, gives the Governor-General powers to be exercised in his own right and powers that can only be exercised on the advice of the Executive Council (essentially Ministers of the Commonwealth Government). According to the Australian Constitution these are powers exercised by the Governor-General.

<u>In The Governor-General's Own Right.</u>

1. The Governor-General is appointed by the Queen as her representative in the Commonwealth and subject to the Constitution, has the powers the Queen assigns to him. Section 2.

2. The Governor-General can only receive the salary of his office. Another paying Commonwealth position is not allowed. Section 4.

3. The Governor-General can appoint times for sessions of Parliament, dissolve the House of Representatives, prorogue (suspend) the Parliament and generally determine when Parliament sits. Sections 5 and 28.

4. When a Senator is chosen (by-election or to fill a casual vacancy) the names are certified by a State Governor to the Governor-General. Sections 7 and 15.

5. The President of the Senate, or the Speaker of the House of Representatives, may resign his seat or office in writing to the Governor-General. Sections 17 and 35.

6. A Senator or member of the House of Representatives may resign, in writing, to the Governor-General if the President of the Senate or the Speaker of the House of Representatives is not available. Sections 19 and 37.

7. If the Senate president is unavailable when a Senate vacancy happens, the Governor-General shall notify the relevant State Governor. Section 21.

8. The Governor-General, or a person authorised by him, receives the oath of affirmation of allegiance from Senators and members of the House of Representatives before they take their Parliamentary seats. Section 42.

9. The Governor-General, via a message, must recommend the purpose for any vote, resolution or proposed law for the appropriation of revenue before it is passed. Section 56.

10. If the two House of Parliament can't agree on the passage of a Bill, the Governor-General can, after certain procedures have been followed, dissolve the Senate and the House of Representatives simultaneously. If a new Parliament is still unable to agree on the proposed legislation, the Governor-General can convene a joint sitting of Parliament. Section 57.

11. Once the Parliament has passed a law, the Governor-General can either assent, withhold assent or reserve the

law for the Queen's pleasure. Furthermore, the Governor-General can return a proposed law to the Parliament with suggested amendments for the House to deal with. Section 58.

12. If the Queen chooses to disallow or reserve a law for consideration, the Governor-General needs to make her decision known to both Houses of Parliament. Sections 59 and 60.

13. The executive power of the Commonwealth is exercisable by the Governor-General as the Queen's representative. Section 61.

14. The Governor-General chooses, summons (and can dismiss) members of the Federal Executive Council. Section 62.

15. The Ministers of State hold office at the pleasure of the Governor-General. Section 64.

16. The Governor-General can decide what offices Ministers of State hold if the Parliament does not. Section 65.

17. The Governor-general is commander-in-chief of the naval and military forces of the Commonwealth. Section 68.

18. The Governor-General decided, after the establishment of the Commonwealth, when the State departments of posts, telegraphs, telephones, naval and military defence, lighthouses, lightships, beacons, buoys and quarantine would be transferred to the Commonwealth. Section 69.

19. A Justice of the High Court, or of a court created by the Parliament, may resign by writing to the Governor-General. Section 72.

20. The Commonwealth Parliament can make laws limiting matters that can be referred to the Queen in Council (Privy Council) but any such laws need to be reserved by the Governor-General for the Queen's pleasure. Section 74.

21. The Governor-General (with authorisation from the Queen) can appoint his deputies. Section 126.

22. Any proposed law for an alteration to the Constitution must be passed by both House of Parliament before submission to voters in a referendum. If agreement is not reached in the Parliament, the Governor-General may submit the law, last proposed by the House in which it originated, to the people. Section 128.

<u>Exercised by the Governor-General on the Advice of the Executive Council (Federal Ministers).</u>

The Governor-General in Council is given the following authority.

1. Issue writs for the general election of members of the House of Representatives. Section 32.

2. Issue writs for an election caused by a vacancy in the House of Representatives if the Speaker of this House is unable to. Section 33.

3. Appoint Ministers of State to administer established departments. Section 64.

4. Assume functions which passed to the executive government of the Commonwealth at Federation and were previously the providence of Colonial (State) Governors. Section 70.

5. The appointment and removal of officers of the Executive Government, other than Ministers of State, can be undertaken by the Governor-General in Council unless the Parliament decides otherwise. Section 67.

6. Appoint (and remove) Justices of the High Court or other courts created by the Parliament. For removal, both Houses of Parliament must address issues of misbehaviour or incapacity. Section 72.

7. Determine how long State departments associated with customs, excise and bounties and transferred to the Commonwealth will remain in the Commonwealth. Section 85.

8. Appoint (and remove) members of the Inter-State Commission. Section 103.

Comments: Does Australia need a Governor-General?

Transitionary Powers

- There are powers of the Governor-General which were relevant soon after Federation and relate to the transfer of

State Departments to the Commonwealth. These sections are redundant as is any role held by a Governor-General in the referral of cases to the British Privy Council. The Privy Council is a body that advises the British Monarch. Historically it became the final court of appeal in the British Colonies mainly to promote unified English common law throughout the British Empire. In 1968 and 1975, 'Privy Council Limitations of Appeals Acts' in Australia limited matters that could be appealed. The 1986, 'Australia Act', passed in Britain and Australia confirmed Australia's independent status from Britain. The United Kingdom could no longer be involved in Australian law making. The Australian High Court is the final Court of appeal.

- The Inter-State Commission no longer exists so appointments by a Governor-General are redundant.

Administration of Government

- Some of the Governor-General's powers may be described as administrative and could be undertaken by the Speaker of the House of Representatives, the President of the Senate, the Chief Justice of the High Court or the Prime Minister (or their representatives). These include; accepting resignations, certifying nominations for elections and taking oaths. Other powers such as issuing writs for elections can be performed by current office holders. The Speaker or Deputy Speaker of the House of Representatives can issue writs for a by-election and a general election is managed by the Electoral Commission. Senate elections are the province of the States but managed by the Electoral Commission.

The Power of an Unelected Official

- The Governor-General is not an elected representative and Australia is supposed to be a democracy. Why have an appointed Governor-General announcing proposed laws associated with the appropriation of revenue (the Public Accounts Committee and Auditor-General are better placed to ensure public money is well spent), refusing to sign or delaying a law passed by both Houses of Parliament (remnants of British surveillance of our legislation), commanding military forces or being involved in deciding whether a proposed law should go to a referendum?

- The last time Royal assent was refused in the United Kingdom was in 1708. The British Sovereign retains the prerogative to refuse assent to Acts passed by the British Parliament but convention dictates that assent is given. There is no reason why the British Monarch or her representative in Australia, the Governor-General, should retain the right to refuse assent to Bills passed by both Houses of the Australian Parliament. This removes any suggestion that behind the scenes influence is exerted on proposed bills by the Monarch or Governor General and upholds the democratic process. An unelected body should not override the decision of an elected Parliament. When a Bill is passed by both Houses of Parliament it automatically becomes law. There is a Federal Register of Legislation (www.legislation.gov.au) which provides the full text of individual laws and their development.

- The Prime Minster is the premier elected member of the governing party. Ministers are appointed and if needs be, dismissed by the Prime Minister. The public service is governed by 'The Public Service Act, 1999'. Employees are responsible to the Australian Parliament by way of their respective Government Ministers. There is no need for a Governor-General to have any role in appointments. They should not hold office at the pleasure of the Governor-General.

- The Australian Parliament is supposed to be a mature organisation and shouldn't need an unelected umpire with nominal powers. If the two Houses of Parliament become deadlocked over a proposed law the Government is determined to pass, the procedures outlined in section 57 of the Constitution could be followed without the need for the Governor-General to dissolve both Houses forcing the country to a double dissolution election. Once the requirements of section 57 are satisfied, the two Houses could come together, at the Prime Minister's direction and the proposed law voted on. The New South Wales 'Consolidation Acts 1902', Section 5A, tackles a possible impasse between the Houses over revenue or moneys bills for the ordinary annual service of the Government by giving the Upper House, the option of suggesting amendments but no option to prevent the ultimate passage of a bill into law (with or without any suggested amendments).

- Section 61 of the Constitution states that the executive power of the Commonwealth is exercisable by the Governor-General as the Queen's representative. The executive branch of the Australian Government consists of the Cabinet and the Ministry led by the Prime Minister. It proposes laws to the Parliament, manages their passage through the Parliament and with the assistance of the public service, executes laws when passed. The Governor-General has no effective political power in this process and must act on the advice of the Executive Government. If the Governor-General ignored advice could this person be accused of political bias? Without Ministers who have the confidence of the House of Representatives, the Governor-General has no executive power. The Governor-General has become a "rubber stamp". A stamp that could be used for a Minister to hide behind. The Governor-General is not responsible to the people but could be persuaded to make a decision a Minister may wish to be shielded from.

- Section 62 sets up the Federal Executive Council to advise the Governor-General who is able to choose and summon members of this Council. In practice, all Ministers of State and Parliamentary Secretaries are members of the Executive Council (section 64), although only current Ministers participate in Council meetings with the Governor-General. This is a ritual left over from times when the British monarch was ceding power to the Parliament. A 'Federal Executive Handbook' is issued by the Department of Prime Minister and Cabinet which also provides the Secretariat for the Executive Council. The Handbook contains guidelines for the preparation of papers by Departmental Officers and Ministerial staff which are presented at Council meetings usually attended by the Governor-General and two Ministers. Issues addressed in the Handbook include; the proclamation of Acts, commissioning of officers of the Australian Defence Forces, authorisation of government overseas borrowing, approval for the compulsory acquisition of land and authorisation for the issue of Treasury Notes. What useful role can an unelected Governor-General play in perusing proposed legislation. This is an elected Minister's responsibility.

- This leaves some of the more contentious powers of the Governor-General. Sections 5 and 28 of the Constitution allow the Governor-General to decide when Parliament sits and allows this person to dissolve or suspend Parliament, effectively dismissing an elected Government along with the Prime Minister. These conventions are the remains of the British Crown's original authority when a Monarch reigned supreme. The official web site of the office of Governor-General (www.gg.gov.au) states the powers which the Governor-General can exercise without or against ministerial advice and calls them 'reserve powers'. These are the power to; appoint a Prime Minister if an election results in a hung Parliament, dismiss a Prime Minister where that person has lost the confidence of the Parliament or has acted unlawfully, and refuse to dissolve the House of Representatives despite a request by the Prime Minister. This web site also makes note of a legal opinion by Sir Maurice Byers QC in relation to the Governor-General's powers under the Constitution. They are seen not as descriptive but prescriptive.

- An unelected Governor-General should not be involved in political processes, especially when this Governor can be dismissed (on advice to the Queen) by a current Prime Minister. It is doubtful whether the Governor-General could enforce these conventions anyway. Even in concert with the Executive Council, does the Governor-General have the skills or experience to know which proposals are constitutional, lawful or appropriate? This is the responsibility of a Minister with access to resources such as the Attorney General's Department and who is responsible to Parliament and the people.

- There is an argument that on occasions there may not be a responsible Minister to advise a Governor-General. In these cases, the Governor-General needs to use 'reserve powers' to solve the situation. These scenarios are more likely to occur in countries subject to political instability. In Australia for example, there may be no responsible Ministers during caretaker periods while an election is taking place and Parliament is not sitting or when a Prime Minister loses the support of the Lower House and refuses to resign or asks the Governor-General to prorogue Parliament to avoid further votes in the House. In these instances, the Governor-General is supposed to step in. However, if this person is guided by conventions so to can an elected Government abide by conventions and solve the problem itself. Parliament has the capacity to resolve its own political impasses. After the 2010 Federal election, Julia Gillard formed a Labor government with the support of the Greens and two independents. Prime Minister Abbot survived a vote of no confidence by his own party in 2015 but was later displaced by Malcolm Turnbull. In 2016, Turnbull used the building watchdog legislation to force a double dissolution. It is well accepted that the political party that commands a majority in the House of Representatives is the party of government and the head of that party becomes the Prime Minister. Great Britain has the same issues with 'reserve powers' (or prerogative powers). They are being reformed or tamed by statutes and manuals of procedure. These include;

- the 'Fixed-term Parliament Act, 2011', which provides for fixed five year terms for Parliamentary general elections (unless certain provisions are met), and,

- the 'Constitutional Reform and Government Act 2010' which sets out regulations for the civil service, places this organisation under the Minister for Civil Service and provides for a Civil Service Code.

- Core conventions of Parliamentary government could be written into the Constitution or managed by Statutes. They then stop being conventions. It will be especially important that the Parliament has control of the political process when Australia becomes a republic. If an elected President was to assume the present role of the Governor-General, there is no guarantee this person would be impartial and independent. There will be no need to for a president to be involved in past political conventions. A ceremonial role is all that is needed.

Ceremonial Role

- If a head-of-state is retained under a republic and a revamped Constitution the present Governor-General's role, according to the official website, 'to encourage, articulate and represent those things that unite Australia as a nation', could be undertaken in a purely ceremonial way, with no potential for involvement in the day-to-day discord of political parties.

Australia should have a Parliamentary Republic with a non-executive, purely ceremonial, President. In a republic the sovereignty is derived from the people not an hereditary monarch in another country (foreign at that).

4. The People

The people receive scant attention in the Constitution apart from their role in electing members of the House of Representative and the Senate.

1. Senators will be directly chosen by the people of a State voting as one electorate (unless the Parliament decides otherwise). In choosing Senators, an elector can only vote once. Sections 7 and 8.
2. House of Representative members will be chosen by the people of the Commonwealth. Section 24.
3. The number of people in a State will determine how many House of Representative members a State will be entitled to. Section 24.
4. If a State law disqualifies persons of any race from voting at elections in their Lower Houses then these people will not be counted when determining the number of seats a State is allocated. Section 25.
5. To qualify as an elector for the Federal House of Representatives (unless the Parliament decides otherwise) a person must be qualified to vote in their State Lower House elections. A person can only vote once. This also applies for the election of Senators. Sections 8, 10 and 30.

6. An adult who has the right to vote at elections for the lower house in a State Parliament cannot be prevented from voting for the Commonwealth Parliament. Section 41.

7. Any person can sue, for the sum of one hundred pound a day, a member of Parliament who sits unlawfully (until the Parliament otherwise provides). Section 46.

8. The Commonwealth Parliament can make laws in the following areas.

   - Regarding marriage, divorce, parental rights and custody of children. Sections 51(xxi) and 51(xxii).

   - For invalid and old age people as well as maternity allowances, pensions and medical and dental benefits. Sections 51(xxiii) and 51(xxiiiA).

   - For the people of any race when this is necessary. Section 51(xxvi).

   - For the acquisition, on just terms, of property from any persons. Section 51(xxxi).

9. The Senate cannot amend any proposed law that would increase a charge or burden on the people. Section 53.

10. The trial of people committing offences against the Commonwealth, on indictment, will be by jury and in the State where the offence occurred. Section 80.

11. The Commonwealth will not curtail the right of any State resident to the reasonable use of river water for irrigation or conservation. Section 100.

12. The Commonwealth cannot legislate against the establishment, observance or exercise of religion. Section 116.

13. A subject of the Queen in one State will not be subject to discrimination or any disability in another State. Section 117.

14. States are responsible for the detention of prisoners who have been convicted of offences against the Commonwealth. Section 120.

15. A State's boundaries can be altered with the approval of the State and a majority of the electors of the State. Section 123.

16. Referendums to alter the Constitution need to be passed by a majority of voters across the Commonwealth and in a majority of States, a majority of voters need to approve of the proposed law. Section 128.

Comments: Does an Australian Constitution need to be more explicit about the rights of citizens?

<u>The People As Electors</u>

- There is no guarantee in the Constitution of the right to vote. Sections 7 and 24 state that the Senate and House of Representatives will be 'directly chosen by the people' but section 30 allows the Parliament to provide the qualification of electors for members of the House of Representatives.

Even more confusingly, section 41 seems to give State law the right to determine who will vote in State elections and therefore Federally. The High Court has ruled that section 41 only applies to people entitled to vote in State elections before a uniform federal franchise was brought in with the 'Commonwealth Franchise Act, 1902'. None of these people would be alive today. The right to vote is probably implied under sections 7 and 24.

- At Federation, the Commonwealth relied on State franchises to determine who could vote Federally but since then, the 'Commonwealth Electoral Act 1918', established the Australian Electoral Commission and details its functions and powers in the organisation of Commonwealth elections for the Senate and House of Representatives. The Commission reports to the Special Minister of State. The Electoral Act lists the basic qualifications of electors as being eighteen years and over and an Australian citizen. Electors are disqualified from voting if serving a prison sentence of three years or more, are convicted of treason, or are unable to understand the voting process.

Protection of Civil Liberties

While the Constitution does provide for the protection of some human rights they are scarce and scattered across the document.

- Section 25 (provisions as to races disqualified from voting) has been labelled racist, particularly against Indigenous Australians. However, it can be seen as protecting voting rights in Australia because if a State disqualifies any voters on the basis of race, these people will not be counted for the purposes of allocating Parliamentary seats to a State. This can act as a disincentive to State's disenfranchising any of the population. Not that any State laws do this.

- If a person believes the Commonwealth has acted unlawfully, the case can be taken to the High Court for review. This has been extended by a High Court decision to State level, via the State's Supreme Court.

- According to section 80, trial by jury only applies to offences against Commonwealth laws. In addition, a charge has to be by indictment (a serious offence such as murder held in a Supreme Court) before a jury is involved. One criticism of section 80, is that the Commonwealth can avoid indictments and prosecute some offences by summary (less serious issues) to be heard before a magistrate rather than a jury. There is also the possibility that an offender must go before a jury, even though the State, in which the person is being prosecuted on behalf of the Commonwealth, allows trial by judge.

- Section 116 prohibits the Commonwealth from establishing any religion, imposing any religious observance, limiting the free exercise of religion or imposing a religious test on

Commonwealth officers. The Constitution does not define 'religion' making it easy for various groups to claim a religious affiliation and it does not prevent the Commonwealth from making laws around religious schools or hospitals or providing religious bodies with exemptions from taxation. Furthermore, the freedom of religion offered in Section 116, applies only to Commonwealth law and is not a national guarantee of religious freedom.

- The protection offered by section 117 which prevents discriminating against citizens from another State makes it easier for people to take their qualifications interstate but has a down-side by reducing a State's freedom to be innovative in its own jurisdiction.

- Section 51(xxxi) offers protection to property owners by guaranteeing acquisition on just terms but fails to stipulate under what conditions and whether the transaction is voluntary.

- The Federal Government can make special laws for people of any race. (section 51(xxvi). These laws can be beneficial as well as detrimental.

- The Commonwealth Parliament has the power to make laws relating to external affairs according to section 51(xxix). This allows the government to use its obligations under international treaties to pass acts that complement these conventions. 'The 'Racial Discrimination Act, 1975', is based on the International Convention on the Elimination of All Forms of Racial Discrimination.

- Section 109 may give citizens protection in some instances because Commonwealth laws prevail over State laws.
- The Parliament can receive petitions from citizens via a Petitions Committee which refers these documents to the relevant Minister for comment.

It can be argued that Australia's system of responsible government and adherence to common law that has evolved over time in Britain and Australia is sufficient protection for citizens. This, along with a number of statutes covering human rights, should preclude any need for a Bill of Rights to be written into the Constitution. The problem being, statutes can be amended and repealed by the Parliament. An expressed difficulty with a Bill of Rights is that an unelected judiciary may be able to have a central role in the interpretation of these rights. A Charter of Human Rights could be written to encourage a rights-based interpretation of the law but courts would not be able to refute laws based on these rights, merely bring inconsistencies to the attention of Parliament.

Australia has a number of Commonwealth Acts aimed at protecting human rights, for example; 'Racial Discrimination Act, 1975', 'Sex Discrimination Act, 1984', the 'Disability Discrimination Act, 1992' and the 'Age Discrimination Act,

1996'. Australia has a Human Rights and Equal Opportunity Commission with responsibility to monitor and promote human rights protection. In addition, there is a Senate Standing Committee for Scrutiny of Bills whose role it is to determine whether bills trespass on personal rights or liberties (although bills are often passed before this Committee can do its work). These Acts, along with human rights protection in the Constitution, common law that shapes court decisions and international law, provide a patchwork of human rights protections. They need to be distilled into a single document.

It is notable that Victoria has a 'Charter of Human Rights and Responsibilities, 2006' and the Australian Capital Territory has 'The Human Rights Act, 2004'. There is no national Charter or Bill of Rights although the Federal Parliament has ratified the 'International Covenant on Civil and Political Rights' and the 'International Covenant on Economic Social and Cultural Rights' with an undertaking to incorporate them into Australian law.

The United Kingdom's 'Human Rights Act, 1998', lists human rights such as; the right to life, prohibition of torture, slavery or forced labour, liberty and security, freedom of thought and religion, prohibition of discrimination and many more. A National Human Rights Consultation Process in Australia produced a report in 2009 which added an extra aspect to the usual list of human rights to be protected. This report urged consideration of those groups in society who are vulnerable and most in need of protection. The elderly, disabled, mentally ill, people living in remote communities, Aboriginal and Torres Strait Islander peoples, children, asylum seekers and new immigrants. The report prioritised education as a way to improve and promote human rights in Australia and recommended an audit of federal legislation, policies and practices as they relate to human rights with a report to Parliament.

An enunciation of human rights in the Australian Constitution would make it clearer to citizens the protections awarded to them instead of the need to interrogate parts of the present Constitution and a variety of Acts passed by the Commonwealth Parliament. Australia is different, racially, culturally and religiously than it was when the present Constitution was drafted.

Human rights issues need to be in a single document, such as a constitution, allowing the public to be more aware of Australia's human rights obligations and protections under the law.

5. The House of Representatives

According to the Australian Constitution this is how the House of Representatives operates.

1. The Federal Parliament's legislative power will be vested in the Queen, a Senate and the House of Representatives. Section 1.
2. The Parliament needs to sit at least once a year. Section 6.
3. Members of the House of Representatives will be directly chosen by the people of the Commonwealth. Section 24.
4. The number of House of Representative members will be as near as possible to twice the number of Senators (with at least five House of Representatives members per State). Section 24.
5. The number of members in the House of Representatives will be in proportion to a State's population. The Parliament can decide how this number is arrived at. The Constitution does suggests a quota is calculated (number of people in the Commonwealth divided by twice the number of senators) and then the number of members per State will be the number of people in a State divided by the quota. Section 24.
6. The Parliament can provide otherwise but the Constitution states that a member of the House of Representatives

should be twenty one years, resident in the Commonwealth for three years and a subject of the Queen. Section 34.

7. A Speaker for the House must be chosen and can be removed by a vote of the House. Section 35.

8. A member of the House of Representatives must take an oath or affirmation of allegiance as prescribed in the Constitution. Section 42.

9. A member of the House of Representatives cannot sit in the Senate. Section 43.

10. Members of the House of Representatives are ineligible to be chosen for or sit in Parliament if they are: a foreign citizen; attainted by treason; subject to, or under sentence for, a gaol term of a year or longer; an undischarged bankrupt; insolvent or can profit from the Crown in addition to their Parliamentary salary and allowances. This last requirement does not apply to Ministers of State, officers of the Queen's navy or army or the Commonwealth's military. Disqualification leads to a vacancy. Sections 44 and 45.

11. If a member of the House of Representatives becomes disqualified to sit, the member can be sued by any person at the rate of one hundred pounds for each ineligible day. Section 46.

12. If there is a dispute over an election, a vacancy or the qualifications of a member of the House of Representatives this House should determine the question. Section 47.

13. Members of the House of Representatives shall receive an allowance of four hundred pound a year (until the Parliament otherwise decides). Section 48.

14. The powers, privileges and immunities of members of the House of Representatives and the order and conduct of the business and proceedings of the House shall be determined by Parliament. Sections 49 and 50.

15. The legislative powers of the Commonwealth Parliament are itemised. Section 51.

16. Proposed laws appropriating revenue or moneys, or imposing taxation can only arise in the House of Representatives. Section 53.

17. Any proposed appropriation law arising in the House of Representatives shall not be considered appropriating revenue or moneys, or to impose taxation if it also has provisions for the imposition or appropriation of fines or other pecuniary penalties. Section 53.

18. If the House of Representatives sends a proposed law to the Senate and this House twice rejects or fails to pass the proposed law, the Governor-General may dissolve both Houses of Parliament. If in a new Parliament, the Senate again rejects the proposed law, the Governor-General can convene a joint sitting of Parliament where members vote, as one, to pass or reject the proposed law. Section 57.

Comments: How well does the Constitution describe the workings of the House of Representatives?

What is the House of Representatives Most Important Role?

- The Commonwealth Government is formed in the House of Representatives and this chamber initiates most legislation. The Constitution has itemised the areas over which the Commonwealth can legislate, assuming the States would continue to legislate in areas they managed before Federation (apart from customs and excise duties which the Commonwealth used to fund its inauguration). This has led to disagreements with the States whose legislative role sometimes overlaps with that of the Commonwealth.
- The Constitution makes a stipulation on laws appropriating revenue. These laws cannot originate in the Senate or be amended by that body and they must deal exclusively with raising revenue or imposing taxation.

What Qualifications Do Members Need to Nominate for the House of Representatives?

- They must not sit in the Senate.
- They need to be twenty-one, a resident in the Commonwealth for three years and a subject of the Queen. Section 34 which deals with the qualifications of a member of the House of Representatives (and the Senate as per section 16) has the clause, 'until the Parliament otherwise

provides'. The Commonwealth Electoral Act, 1918 (sections 70, 93, 99, 163 and 164 of this Act) sets out the qualifications needed to be nominated for a place in Parliament. They are; aged eighteen years, an Australian citizen, able to vote in the House of Representatives and Senate elections and not a member of a State or Territory Parliament.

- Under Section 44 of the Constitution: A candidate for either House of Parliament can be disqualified and their position declared vacant if, at nomination for a seat;
  - they have allegiance, obedience or adherence to a foreign power,
  - they are a subject, citizen or entitled to the rights of a foreign power,
  - attainted (touched) by treason,
  - under or subject to a gaol sentence of one year or more,
  - they are an undischarged bankrupt,
  - hold a pension from the Commonwealth and hold any office that profits under the Crown (except Ministers of State and officers of the Queen's navy or army), and,
  - have any pecuniary interest in the Public Service of the Commonwealth unless this involves an incorporated company with more than twenty five members.
- Section 44 is essentially about disqualifying a member of Parliament who has a conflict of interest or who may be of doubtful character. Since 2017, members of both Houses of

Parliament need to sign a citizenship register confirming their Australian citizenship and provide evidence of any necessary renunciation or attempted renunciation.

- The High Court's principal test on citizenship under the Constitution is that; 'all steps that could be reasonably taken to renounce any foreign nationality or citizenship' must be taken. This makes it difficult for Australian citizens of foreign decent and people who have foreign citizenship conferred on them without their knowledge. The Senate Standing Committee on Constitutional and Legal Affairs Report (1981), recommended that section 44(i) which deals with the citizenship issue, be deleted and replaced by a provision in the Electoral Act regarding the consequences of foreign allegiance. Any person who made a declaration that they had taken all reasonable steps to divest themselves of foreign nationality could nominate for a seat. They could not take any conscious advantage of any right or entitlement arising from unsought nationality whilst in office.

- If the issue of citizenship was more clearly spelled out there would be less need for the expensive involvement of the High Court. A revised Constitution would provide an opportunity to remove some of the current vagueness and irrelevancies such as; what if citizenship is conferred unbeknown on a person, or what is a foreign power? States may have different sentencing laws. A sentence of one year or more in one State may equate to a sentence of six months in another and it is puzzling why employees of large companies and the Queen's military officers are offered exemptions from disqualification.

- Dual citizenship in this multicultural society could be allowed. Otherwise too many Australians are disqualified from entering Parliament and it is up to other nations how readily a second citizenship can be revoked. The Constitution also reduces the number of Australians who can nominate for election to Parliament because Government workers such as teachers, university lecturers, police officers and military personnel need to leave employment whilst they campaign for a seat (section 44(iv)). This makes it a gamble for many Australians. Section 32 of the 'Public Service Act, 1999' does provide public servants with the right to return to their job if unsuccessful at an election. This does not take into account Local Government personnel. Section 44(iv) also makes it difficult for Senators-elect who may have to wait months, without employment, before taking their seat. Members could take leave from employment after successful nomination for a seat in Parliament but only relinquish this employment from the moment they are entitled to a Parliamentary salary.

- There is also a need to recognise that too many restrictions on member qualifications can be used by party politics to remove members (especially when the Government has a slim majority).

- To take matters out of the hands of the High Court and foreign governments, Parliament could decide the qualifications and disqualifications of Federal politicians. It is interesting to note the pledge given under the 'Australian Citizenship Act 1984', which is: *'From this time forward (under God) I pledge my loyalty to Australia and its people whose democratic beliefs I share, whose rights and liberties I respect, and whose laws I will uphold and obey'*. Could the present requirement to hold Australian citizenship be an adequate test of loyalty for politicians?

How Are Elections Conducted?

- The Constitution does not provide any guidance as to how elections are conducted although it does state that members of Parliament are chosen by the people of the Commonwealth. The 'Commonwealth Electoral Act, 1918', sets out procedures for the Australian Electoral Commission to follow during elections for both the Senate and the House of Representatives. This Commission also determines electoral boundaries in each State and Territory and hence the number of politicians. Section 27 gives the Parliament the power to determine the number of members of the House of Representatives (and hence the Senate).

<u>What Happens if an Unqualified Member is Elected?</u>

- Section 47 of the Constitution, allows any disputed election to be resolved in the House 'in which the question arises'. However, this Section comes with the familiar 'until the Parliament otherwise provides'. It would seem the Parliament would rather the High Court sort out disqualifications than bear the responsibility itself. Perhaps this is because Section 45 deals with the consequences of disqualification under the Constitution. The seat will be declared vacant but the Constitution does not provide guidance on how breaches are to be dealt with before declaring a seat vacant. A citizen, or the Parliament, can use the 'Commonwealth Electoral Act, 1918' (sections 354, 355 and 376) to refer disputes about members' eligibility to sit, to the High Court (which sits as the Court of Disputed Returns).

<u>Can a Disqualified Member be Financially Penalised for Time Spent 'Illegally' in Parliament?</u>

- Section 46 deals with the monetary consequences of becoming ineligible to retain a seat in Parliament. This section makes a disqualified member liable to pay a penalty for every day the seat should have been declared vacant. However, the Section comes with the phrase; 'until the Parliament otherwise provides' and it has done that. The 'Common Informers (Parliamentary Disqualifications) Act,

1975', which was amended in 2008, makes it clear that a member of parliament is not liable to pay.

<u>Oath of Allegiance</u>

- When a new Parliament is formed, members elected to the House of Representatives (and the Senate) must swear an oath or affirm an allegiance to the Crown. The oath is in the Schedule to the Constitution. It reads: *'I, A. B. do swear that I will be faithful and bear true allegiance to Her Majesty Queen Victoria, Her heirs and successors according to law. So Help Me God.* Or members can, *'solemnly and sincerely affirm and declare that I ...'* The oath is usually administered by a Justice of the High Court on authorisation of the Governor-General.

- Section 62 of the Constitution states that members of the Federal Executive Council will be sworn in as Executive Councillors by the Governor-General. These Ministers make an oath as a member of Parliament and again at a Ministerial swearing in. There is no specified oath for Ministers and Parliamentary Secretaries and the Prime Minister probably sets the words. This means the oath or affirmation has varied. For example, Prime Minister Gillard declared *'to solemnly and sincerely affirm and declare that I will well and truly serve the Commonwealth of Australia in the office of Prime Minister'*. Prime Minister Abbott, on the other-hand, declared that *'I do swear that I will well and truly serve the people of Australia in the office of Prime Minister and I will be faithful and bear true allegiance to her Majesty Queen Elizabeth the Second, Queen of Australia. So help me God'*. Ministers probably follow the example of their Prime Minister.

- As an independent nation, the Australian people are sovereign. This oath would be reworded under a Republic where there is an opportunity to swear allegiance to Australia and renounce any other allegiances. After the 1998 Constitutional Convention, a bill, 'The Constitution Alteration (Establishment of Republic Bill) Bill, 1999', suggested the oath ' *Under God I swear that I will be loyal to the Commonwealth of Australia and the Australian People, whose laws I will uphold'* or 'I *solemnly and sincerely affirm that I will ….'*. The West Australian Constitution allow the oath or affirmation; '*I will faithfully serve the people of Western Australia as a member of the Legislative Council/Legislative Assembly'*.

What Are Members Paid?

- The Constitution allows four hundred pounds per year payable to members of the House of Representatives and Senate and up to twelve thousand pounds a year for Ministers of State. The Parliament is allowed to provide otherwise and the 'Parliamentary Business Resources Act 1952 ' provides for resources payable to current and some past members of the Commonwealth Parliament. This Act sets out guidelines for members on how resources are to be used for the purpose of conducting Parliamentary business. The Renumeration Tribunal, established under the 'Renumeration Tribunal Act, 1973', determines the salary, allowances and entitlements payable to members.

<u>How Many Members Are in the House of Representatives?</u>

- The number of members in the House of Representatives is determined by the population of the States. The Electoral Commission relies on periodic Census data and the advice of the Commonwealth Statistician to determine the number of electors in the Commonwealth and the States and Territories. People are represented in proportion to their State's population so that each member will have approximately the same number of citizens in their electorates. This requires occasional redistributions. The Parliament can decide on a calculation for determining membership but the Constitution offers a possible solution in section 24 which is followed by the Commission. At present, there are 150 members in the House of Representatives.
- The 'Ministers of State Act 1952', sets out the allowable number of Commonwealth Ministers at 42. At present, there are 30 Ministers of State and 12 Parliamentary Secretaries. They come mainly from the House of Representatives but a small number of Ministers sit in the Senate.

Are There Standards of Behaviour for Members?

- The Constitution allows each House of Parliament to make its own rules with regard to the order and conduct of its business and proceedings. In the House of Representatives, the Prime Minister issues a 'Statement of Ministerial Standards' where Ministers are encouraged to be accountable and to act with integrity and fairness. All in the name of advancing the public interest. Soon after swearing-in, members of Parliament must complete a 'Register of Members Interests'. This lists the member's interests and those of close family members and dependents. There is also a 'Register of Lobbyists' and a code of conduct for these people in an attempt to provide transparency in their dealings with Commonwealth Government employees.

What Powers and Privileges Do Members Have?

- The Constitution allows the powers, privileges and immunities of members to be determined by Parliament (Section 49). 'The Parliamentary Privileges Act, 1987', sets out these responsibilities for members of both Houses of the Parliament and includes;
- the circumstances under which freedom of speech is protected during debates, committee work or for tabled documents and petitions,

- penalties that can be imposed for an offence against the House, and,
- the inability of a House to expel a member and the protection of witnesses giving evidence before the House.

The Act also covers the ability of a House to impose a penalty of imprisonment or a fine for offences against the House but it prohibits the expulsion of a member from membership of a House and provides immunity from arrest whilst the House is sitting. Section 49 gives the Parliament considerable authority and citizens may want some say in the scope of such privileges and immunities. Something they have never been given.

- Citizens, who feel they have a grievance about remarks made in Parliament can make a written submission to the Speaker of the House of Representatives and ask that responses be on the Parliamentary record. The Speaker can refer such matters to the Committee of Privilege and Members' interests.

- Since 1984, for the House of Representatives and 1994 for the Senate, members must disclose significant family financial interests. The House of Representatives Standing and Sessional Orders provide for a Committee of Members' interests to be appointed at the start of a new Parliamentary session.

How Often Does the House of Representatives Sit?

- In the last twenty years, the House of Representatives has sat for an average of 65 days a year and the Senate for 56 days. There seems little point in dictating sitting days since time spent in Parliament is dependent on factors such as; the legislative program, the time of each sitting and whether it is an election year. Current sessions are well in excess of the Constitution's specification of a yearly event. It may be worth stipulating that no more than six months can pass before a Parliamentary sits.

How Does the House of Representatives Conduct its Business?

- The House can determine the conduct of its business, often in concert with the Senate. This has led to legislation such as; the 'Parliamentary Papers Act, 1908' (rules governing the publication of Parliamentary papers), 'Parliamentary Proceedings Broadcasting Act, 1946-73' (deals with the broadcast of Parliamentary proceedings), the 'Parliamentary Precincts Act, 1988' (relates to the management of Parliament House property), and the 'Parliamentary Services Act 1999' (the management of Parliamentary staff). The House of Representatives (and the Senate) also have Standing Orders. The Orders for the House of Representatives cover; the election of the Speaker and the management of this Office, quorum requirements, question time, management of Bills, voting procedures and conduct of committees. Orders for the Senate include; management of the Office of the President of the Senate, instructions for committees and the scrutiny of Bills, attendance of senators, quorum requirements and the treatment of petitions. The above Acts and Standing Orders give both houses of Parliament additional authority to that offered in the Constitution and the Orders can be changed.

How is the House of Representative Dissolved?

- The House of Representative is supposed to continue for three years but can be dissolved sooner by the Governor-General. This is a significant decision because dissolution of the lower house effectively shuts down Parliament. The Governor-General can also determine when sessions are held and can suspend Parliament. The Constitution does not give the conditions under which sittings of the House of Representative are determined and the Governor-General does not have to make public reasons for any decisions to suspend or dismiss this House. A Governor-General has not ignored a Prime Minister's advice on the dissolution of Parliament since 1909. In practice, the Prime Minister determines when Parliament sits.

What if the Senate and the House of Representatives are Deadlocked over a Proposed Law?

- Section 57 sets out an expensive and time consuming way to solve a deadlock between the two Houses of Parliament because it can result in the Governor-General calling a double dissolution of Parliament and the possibility that any new Parliament will be similarly constituted. Politicians do not welcome an election, especially if it is soon after the last and voters elect a government to get on with it and manage its legislative programme. It is likely that a deadlock has political party overtures, especially when the government does not control the Senate. The Governor-General should not be involved in a party dispute. Also, as it stands, Section 57 seems at odds with Section 5 where the Governor-General decides sessions of Parliament, whereas Section 57 allows a deadlocked Parliament to decide. The quickest resolution is for the two Houses to have a joint sitting, without the need for a new election and vote as a block to solve the deadlock. The Indian Constitution (Article, 108, Legislative Procedure) breaks a deadlock in this way as does the Victorian Constitution (Constitution Act, 1975).

- In New South Wales, if the disagreement between the Houses of Parliament relates to the appropriation of revenue, the NSW Constitution (Constitution Act 1902 No 32) allows the upper house (Legislative Council) to examine appropriation Bills but if this House fails to pass the Bill within a certain time, it automatically becomes law". The 1988 Commission on Constitutional Reform suggested: ' if at any time during the first three years of a Parliament the Senate rejects, or fails to pass, within thirty days of its transmission, a Bill it cannot amend, the Bill, shall be presented for Royal assent'. The above procedures mitigate against the Senate denying financial resources to a Government simply to force it to an election.

- A fixed term in office of three or four years for the House of Representatives would mean there could not be an early election for this House unless certain conditions were met. The States of New South Wales, Victoria, South Australia, Western Australia and the Australian Capital Territory have four year fixed-term Parliaments. This provides for longer term planning and some certainty to Parliamentary members and the public.

- Another alternative is to permit departments and agencies to spend at last year's allocation of funds until a stalled revenue bill is resolved. This could stop deadlocks being used for short term political gain. Senator Macklin, in 1987, under the 'Constitutional Alteration (Appropriations for the Ordinary Annual Services of the Government) Bill', suggested:

'if the House of Representatives passes a proposed law appropriating revenue for the ordinary annual service of Government and if the Senate has not passed the law after sixty days, then until the situation is resolved, a law comes into force allowing the expenditure of last years appropriated amount'.

What Does the Constitution Fail to Mention About the House of Representatives?

- The role of political parties in the House (apart from a mention in section 15 where a Senate casual vacancy can be filled by a member of the same political party) and the importance of party discipline to stable government does not feature. Nor does the Constitution tell how a Government is formed in the House of Representatives from the majority party or a coalition of parties which elect the Prime Minister.

- There is no mention of the role of the Opposition, as the largest minority party, in holding the Government to account by participation in debates, committees and question times in order to scrutinise proposed legislation and suggest changes. There is no reference to the role played by the Opposition Leader in the House of Representatives or the Shadow Cabinet.

- The function of the Cabinet and the leadership of the Prime Minister. is not spelled out. The fact that most policy decisions are made in the Cabinet and the importance of Cabinet solidarity around decisions is not mentioned. The Cabinet Handbook sets out aspects such as; the roles and responsibilities of Ministers, conventions, the management of meetings, the conduct of business and the security of documents. Given Cabinet members are chosen by the Prime Minister as an administrative body to help the decision making processes of Government, it may not need to be provided for in the Constitution.

- The appointment of Ministers of State (mainly from the House of Representatives but also from the Senate) is part of the Constitution but not their allocation to portfolios and their responsibilities in the administration of departments and other agencies. There is no mention of whether Ministers need to accept personal responsibility for the actions of their departments. Nor any mention of how all Ministers resign their portfolios if the Prime Minister loses office for some reason (death, resigns, loses party or House support, calls a new election). The central role of the Treasurer in the House of Representatives, as the only House that can initiate financial legislation, is not covered in the Constitution.

- A caretaker government usually occurs between the dissolution of the House of Representatives and the results of a general election. The Department of the Prime Minister publishes 'The Guidance of Caretaker Conventions'. This document outlines the responsibilities of a caretaker government not to enter into contracts or make policy decisions that would impact on an incoming government, to refrain from making appointments or dismissing personnel, not to involve government employees in political activities and generally just keep government ticking over. This is an important hiatus in government but receives no constitutional mention.

6. The Senate

According to the Australian Constitution this is how the Senate operates.

1. The Federal Parliament's legislative power will be vested in the Queen, a Senate and the House of Representatives. The Senate has the same powers as the House of Representatives to propose laws except for laws dealing with the appropriation of revenue or the imposition of taxation. However, such proposals can be rejected and returned to the House of Representatives with suggested changes. Sections 1 and 53.
2. The Senators will be elected by voters of a State so that members of the Senate represent a State rather than individual electorates. They hold office for six years. Section 7.
3. The Parliament can decide on the number of Senators per State so long there are at least six Senators per State and the numbers remain equal. The method of choosing Senators lies with the Commonwealth Parliament. Sections 7 and 9.
4. State Parliaments can make laws to determine the times and places of elections for State Senators. Whatever procedures occur for the election of State lower house

members can be used to elect Senators. The Governor of a State can issue writs for Senate elections. Sections 9, 10, 12 and 14.

5. The Senate can operate if a State fails to send members. Section 11.

6. After a double dissolution involving the Senate, members are divided into two groups. One to serve three years and an equal sized group to serve six years. These Senators take up their seats on the first of July preceding the election. Section 13.

7. In a normal three years election cycle, Senators serve six years (causing half-Senate elections) and Senators take up seats on the first of July after the election. Section 13.

8. Senate vacancies are notified to State Governors and filled by a person of the same political party if possible. Sections 15 and 21.

9. Qualifications to nominate for election to the Senate and House of Representatives are the same. Section 16.

10. The Senate must elect a President and choose a replacement for times when the President is absent. Sections 17 and 18.

11. A Senator may resign by writing to the President or the Governor-General if the President is absent. Section 19.

12. A Senator's seat will become vacant if absent from Parliament, without permission, for two consecutive months. Section 20.

13. To make up a quorum at least one-third of the Senators need to be present, unless the Parliament provides otherwise. Section 22.

14. Each Senator has one vote and questions are resolved by a majority of votes. The President has one vote but if the votes are tied, the issue is lost. Section 23.

15. Before taking a seat in Parliament, each Senator must make an oath or affirmation of allegiance. Section 42.

16. A sitting Senator cannot be chosen for the House of Representatives. Section 43.

17. Senate seats may be lost over the same disqualifications and consequences that apply to members of the House of Representatives. Sections 44, 45, 46 and 47.

18. Senators receive four hundred pounds a year, the same as members of the House of Representatives (unless the Parliament decides otherwise). Section 48.

19. As with the House of Representatives, the powers and privileges of Senators can be decided by Parliament. Section 49.

20. Proposed laws dealing with revenue or monies or taxation cannot originate in the Senate. Nor can the Senate amend such laws pertaining to the annual service of Government although it can suggest alterations. Section 53.

21. The Senate cannot amend any proposed law so as to increase charges or create a burden on the people. Section 53.

22. The Senate can give cause for a double dissolution election if this House refuses to pass a proposed law on two occasions separated by three months. Section 57.

There are Sections of the Constitution which apply equally to Senators and members of the House of Representatives. These are;

- qualifications required to nominate for a seat in Parliament,
- why disqualification of a seat in Parliament might apply and subsequent penalties,
- oaths of allegiance sworn by elected members before taking a Parliamentary seat,
- powers and privileges allocated to members of Parliament,
- the ability of both Houses to determine how they will conduct business, and,
- resolution of deadlocks between the two Houses over proposed bills.

Comments: How well does the Constitution describe the workings of the Senate?

<u>What is the Role of the Senate?</u>
- Senate review of proposed legislation forces the Government to negotiate and compromise. This is an important feature of a democratic government where the consent of both Houses is required to pass legislation.

- This House can amend legislation, except for financial bills concerned with appropriating revenue or imposing taxation. For other bills, the Senate has the right not to pass them unless amended to its satisfaction or to not pass a bill at all.

- The Senate cannot amend a proposed law to increase any charge or burden on the people. It can initiate non financial legislation.

- The Senate makes extensive use of a committee system where legislation can be assessed.

<u>How are Senators Elected?</u>

- Senators are elected by proportional representation. This can result in the election of minor parties on a small proportion of the national vote.

- Senators hold seats for six years. When there is an election for the House of Representatives, usually after three years, half the Senators are up for re-election. Section 13 of the Constitution allows elections for the Senate to be held one year before seats are due to turn over. This is designed to provide flexibility, so both Houses go to an election at the same time, given the House of Representatives can be dissolved at any time. A double dissolution election means all Senators relinquish their seats. In the new Parliament, after a double dissolution, about half the Senate receives a three year term and the rest a six year term. Proposals to synchronise the elections of both Houses of Parliament have failed four times at referendums. This result could be a recognition that the Senate should have a measure of autonomy on election timing. According to Section 12 of the Constitution, the States can make laws to determine the management of Senate elections. In practice they work in with a Commonwealth timetable.

- Terms for Senators representing the Australian Capital Territory and the Northern Territory have an election cycle that matches that of the House of Representatives.

- If a vacancy occurs, an amendment to the Constitution in 1977, means a replacement Senator is of the same political party as an outgoing Senator if this is possible. This is the only time the Constitution mentions political parties. The Senate was supposed to be a States' House but now there is an acknowledgement that adherence to a political party may be more important that allegiance to a State.

How Many Senators are in the House?

- The 'Senate Representation Act, 1983', was an Act to increase the number of Senators. There are 12 Senators representing each State. The 'Commonwealth Electoral Act' sets the number of Senators in the Australian Capital Territory and the Northern Territory at 2 each. The number of Senators is half that of the members of the House of Representatives. There was a total of seventy six senators in 2018.

<u>When does the Senate Sit?</u>

- In 2017 there were 56 sitting days. There is a published register of members' attendance.

A reader of the Australian Constitution should gain a good idea of the powers of the House of Representatives and the Senate and how the Houses are staffed and operated. Some of the workings of Parliament are described by the Constitution but other procedures have been legislated for or otherwise developed. These need to be drawn together in a revised constitution.

7. Where the Parliament Can Decide

There are large sections of the Commonwealth Constitution where the Parliament can make decisions or enact laws without having to go to a referendum to change the Constitution. These Sections of the Constitution are as follows and sometimes written with the rider 'until the Parliament otherwise provides'.

1. The sum of the annual salary of the Governor-General. Section 3.
2. Whether Queensland is permitted to divide the State into divisions for Senate elections rather than voting as a whole like the other States. Section 7.
3. The number of Senators for each State. Section 7.
4. The qualifications of electors for the Senate and House of Representatives. Sections 8, 30 and 31.
5. The method of choosing Senators. Sections 9 and 10.
6. Maintaining an even representation of Senators across States. Section 14.
7. Deciding on a quorum for the Senate. Section 22.
8. How the number of House of Representative members per State will be determined. Sections 24 and 29.
9. The qualifications of a member of the House of Representatives. Section 34.

10. Numbers for a quorum in the House of Representatives. Section 39.

11. Any monetary penalty for sitting in Parliament when disqualified. Section 46.

12. The resolution of disputed qualifications to sit in Parliament. Section 47.

13. The allowance payable to members of Parliament. Section 48 and 66.

14. The powers, privileges and immunities of members of Parliament. Section 49.

15. Rules and orders for the conduct of business in the Parliament. Section 50.

16. The Parliament, subject to the Constitution, has the power to make laws in a number of listed areas. Specifies that the power to make laws with respect to trade and commerce extends to navigation and shipping and to railways the property of any State. Sections 51, 98 and 102.

17. The Commonwealth Government, subject to the Constitution, has exclusive powers to make laws over its property and has control of the public service. Section 52.

18. The number of Ministers of State and the offices they hold. Section 65.

19. The sum payable to Ministers of State. Section 66.

20. The appointment and removal of officers of the Executive Government who are not Ministers. Section 67.

21. The Parliament can create Federal Courts (other than the High Court). Section 71.

22. The number of Justices, in addition the Chief Justice, in the High Court. Section 71.

23. The remuneration of Judges of the High Court and other Federal Courts which cannot be reduced during a term in office. Section 72.

24. The age at which the above Justices retire. Section 72.

25. The High Court's jurisdictions can be subject to exceptions and regulations by the Parliament. Section 73.

26. The conditions of and restrictions on appeals to the Queen in Council from the Supreme Courts of the States. Section 73.

27. Parliament may define the jurisdiction of Federal Courts other than the High Court. Section 77.

28. Determining the number of judges in Commonwealth courts. Section 79.

29. The location of trials for offences against the Commonwealth that were not committed in any State. Section 80.

30. How Commonwealth revenue from duties of customs and excise will be shared with the States. Sections 87, 93, 94 and 97.

31. The terms and conditions regarding financial assistance to the States. Section 96.

32. The powers and administration of the Inter-State Commission and remuneration of its officers. Sections 101 and 103.

33. The Parliament may take over the management of State debts. Sections 105 and 105A.

34. The Commonwealth Parliament may make laws regarding State incarceration of persons convicted on the laws of the Commonwealth. Section 120.

35. The Parliament may establish new States under its terms and conditions. Sections 121 and 122.

36. The seat of Government, in New South Wales, to be determined by the Commonwealth Parliament. Section 125.

Comments: How the Parliament has decided.

<u>Remuneration</u>

- The Remunerations tribunal (three part-time members, 2018) is set up under the 'Remuneration Tribunal Act, 1973'. It is an independent statutory body that advises on the salary, allowances and entitlements for members of the Commonwealth Parliament, other Parliamentary officers, the Federal judiciary, Secretaries of departments and other public officers.

<u>Elections for the House of Representatives and the Senate</u>

- The 'Commonwealth Electoral Act, 1918', established the Australian Electoral Commission which carries out the requirements of the Act. The Commission sets out; qualifications and disqualifications for voters, establishment and maintenance of electoral divisions, management of electoral rolls, registration of political parties, qualifications to nominate for a seat in the Parliament, issuing of writs for elections, management of the voting and counting process, disclosures of election funding and the resolution of elections disputed via the Court of Disputed Returns.

- There have been calls to make voting in Senate elections more transparent. 'Above-the-line-voting' can be chosen by electors. Here a vote is given to a single candidate and preferences flow automatically without the voter necessarily being aware of where their preferences are going. This does save electors from voting 'below the line' where all candidates must be numbered in order of preference for a valid vote. The 'Commonwealth Electoral (Above-the-Line-Voting) Amendment Bill 2008', was introduced to the Federal Parliament by the Greens Party in 2008 and 2010. This Bill was designed to make preference voting easier and more transparent. It has not been passed.

Number of Ministers of State and their Appointment

- The 'Ministers of State Act, 1952', sets the number of Minsters at 42. Twelve Parliamentary Secretaries and 30 other Ministers.

- Federal Ministers and Parliamentary Secretaries are, in practice, appointed and dismissed by the Prime Minister who also allocates an area of responsibility to these persons. They, along with the Prime Minister, form the executive arm of government.

Conduct and Management of Business in the Senate and House of Representatives

- The way the Senate and the House of Representatives manage business is set out in their 'Standing Orders' which are regularly updated.

- There are numerous Acts designed to facilitate the conduct of business in the Houses and the Parliamentary precinct. These include the: 'Parliamentary Papers Act, 1908'; 'Parliamentary Proceedings Broadcasting Act, 1974'; 'Parliamentary Privileges Act, 1987'; 'Parliamentary Services Act, 1999'; 'Parliamentary Resources Act, 2017', and many more.

- The Parliament has prepared documents such as; 'Australian Governments Lobbyist Register', a 'Statement of Ministerial Standards' where members reveal financial interests and a 'Guidance on Caretaker Conventions'.

<u>Financial Penalty for Sitting When Ineligible</u>

- The 'Common Informers (Parliamentary Disqualification) Act, 1975' removes any financial liability from such a member.

<u>Control of the Public Service</u>

- The Australian Public Service Commission is an agency within the Prime Minister and Cabinet portfolio (Minister assisting the Prime Minister for the Public Service) and is established under the 'Public Service Act, 1999'. The Commission sets a 'Code of Conduct' for the service and manages employment policies and training for public servants as well as building the capabilities of the service. The Australian Public Service manages service delivery (police, health, social welfare), taxation collection and management of government finances as well as providing policy advice to the Government.
- It has been suggested that Commonwealth Ministerial staff come under the Public Service Code of Conduct.

<u>Creation of Federal Courts other than the High Court</u>

- The Parliament has legislated for the: Federal Court of Australia under the 'Federal Court of Australia Act, 1976'; Family Court of Australia via the 'Family Law Act, 1975' and the Federal Circuit Court of Australia under the 'Federal Circuit Court of Australia Act, 1999'.

Appeals to the Queen in Council (Privy Council)

- Routes of appeal to the British Privy Council have been closed down by successive Acts. The 'Privy Council (Limitation of Appeals) Act, 1968' and the 'Privy Council (Appeals from the High Court) Act, 1975', meant appeals to the Privy Council involving Federal legislation was closed off. The 'Australia Act, 1986', removed any appeals from a State Supreme Court to the Privy Council. In theory, appeals from the High Court to the Privy Council can be made in inter se matters (dispute between the Commonwealth and one or more States concerning their respective powers). However, the High Court has indicated that it would not do this.

Parliament's Limitations on the High Court

- Section 73 of the Constitution deals with the appellate jurisdiction of the High Court and allows that jurisdiction to be limited *with such exception and subject to such regulation as Parliament prescribes*'. The Parliament has prescribed limitations via section 35A of the 'Judiciary Act 1903'. This requires special leave to appeal which is granted only when a question of law is raised that is of public importance or involves a conflict between courts. However, it is Justices of the High Court who decide whether special leave is granted, so the High Court effectively decides which appeal cases it will consider.

- Section 76 of the Constitution allows the Parliament to remove the inclusion of Constitutional matters from the High Court's remit. A 1998 Constitutional Review recommended an amendment to the Constitution to prevent this occurring. However, section 30 of the 'Judiciary Act 1903', has removed uncertainty by stating that the High Court will have original jurisdiction in *'all matters arising under the Constitution or involving its interpretation'*.

8. Prescribed Parliamentary Powers

<u>Legislative Powers of the Parliament</u>

- Section 51 of the Constitution sets out areas where the Commonwealth Parliament can make laws. At Federation, the States were operating as independent entities and presumably the Commonwealth needed to carve out areas of responsibility, leaving the States with the rest. The Commonwealths responsibilities fall under the following categories.

- the **economy and finance**; taxation, Commonwealth borrowing, currency, coinage, legal tender, paper money, Commonwealth banking and insurance, bills of exchange and promissory notes, bankruptcy and insolvency.
- **trade**; with other countries and among the States, bounties on production or export of goods.
- **military**; naval and military defence of the Commonwealth and the States.
- **business**; foreign corporations, trading and financial corporations formed in the Commonwealth, copyrights and patents, weights and measures.
- **navigation**; lighthouses, lightships, beacons and buoys.
- **immigration**; naturalisation and aliens, immigration and emigration.

- **transport**; control railways for military purposes, acquisition, construction, extension of State railways with their permission.
- **overseas**; external affairs, relationship of the Commonwealth with Pacific Islanders.
- **industrial relations**; conciliation and arbitration of industrial disputes.
- **criminal process**; service and execution in the Commonwealth of the civil and criminal process, judgements of courts of States,
- **special laws**; for people of any race,
- **social support**; marriage, divorce, parental rights, custody and guardianship of infants, invalid and old age pensions, maternity allowances, widows' pensions, child endowment, unemployment benefits, pharmaceutical and hospital benefits, medicinal dental services, student benefits, family allowances, laws for people of any race where deemed necessary, acquisition of property on just terms.
- **utilities and other services**; astronomical and meteorological observations, quarantine, fisheries, census and statistics, postal, telegraphic, telephone and other services.
- After listing the above aspects where the Commonwealth Parliament can enact laws, Section 51(xxxvi) states, 'matters in respect of which this Constitution makes provision until the Parliament otherwise provides'. This is a wide ranging

statement and suggests all of Section 51 (Legislative powers of the Parliament) and more, is subject to laws by the Parliament.

Comments: Some implications of powers given to the Commonwealth Parliament at Federation.

Marriage

- Although the Federal Government had Constitutional authority over marriage, States could have their own rules on marriage until the 'Marriage Act, 1961'. This Act has been amended as society's views have changed to allow celebrants to officiate, ministers to act according to their religious views and to denote marriage as a union between two people rather than necessarily a man and a women.

Social Services

- In 1946 Australians voted, via a referendum, in favour of the, 'Constitutional Alteration (Social Services) Bill' which extended Commonwealth powers over a number of social services (inserted as Section 51(xxiiiA) in the Constitution). The only social service mentioned before this was Section 51(xxiii) relating to invalid and old-age pensions. The 1946 bill was amended in 1947 as the 'Social Services Consolidation Act'. Some issues had already been covered;

the basic wage in 1908, child endowment payments, 1941, widows' pensions, 1942 and unemployment benefits, 1945.

- The Commonwealth Department of Social Services, under the Minister for Social Services, is responsible for the development and delivery of a wide range of services. The most prominent being through Centrelink and Medicare.

Special Laws for Peoples of any Race

- Section 51(xxvi) was originally worded: *'the people of any race, other than the aboriginal race in any State for whom it is deemed necessary to make special laws'*. In its present form (after a referendum in 1967), the Section allows the Commonwealth to make laws in respect of Aboriginal and Torres Strait Islander peoples. However, the Section has the potential for discrimination as well as advancement. It allowed the Commonwealth Parliament to suspend the Racial Discrimination Act and enact the Northern Territory National Emergency Response, 2007 ('the intervention'). On the other hand, it has given the Commonwealth, in cooperation with the States and Territories, the ability to pass legislation such as 'Aboriginal Land Rights (NT) Act, 1976' and the 'Native Title Act, 1993'.

- The Indigenous Law Centre suggested in 2011, that Section 51(xxvi) be reworded as, 'make laws for the peace, order and good governance of the Commonwealth with respect to Aboriginal and Torres Strait Islanders peoples'. A further suggestion is; 'the Commonwealth, a State or a Territory shall not discriminate on the grounds of race, colour or ethnic or national origin'. This does not preclude the making of laws or measures for the purposes of overcoming disadvantage, ameliorating the effects of past discrimination, or protecting cultures, languages or heritage of any group'.

- The concept of race, given Australia's multicultural society, probably has no part in the Constitution.

Trade and Commerce

- Sections 86 to 95 come under 'Finance and Trade' in the Constitution. These Sections were designed to facilitate the transition of the States into the Commonwealth and to give the Commonwealth the revenue it would need to finance its responsibilities. Before Federation, the States received most of their income from customs and excise duties which were not uniform across the States. Under the 'Constitution Act of 1901', the States gave up their right to levy customs and excise duties and bounties and all goods traded between the States were duty free at the borders. Although provisions were made to return some revenue to the States they were left in a financially weakened position.

- In essence, the Federal Government was given exclusive powers to collect and control customs, excise and bounties (i.e. to operate a single tariff policy). The States could not impose taxes on locally produced or imported goods because this could go against a uniform tariff and make it difficult to implement free trade amongst the States. However, bounties could be applied by a State on the mining of gold, silver or other metals.

- The Constitution can be confusing in the use of the terms, excise, customs duties and bounties. In Section 93, customs duties are those applied to goods imported into a State and afterwards passing into another State, whereas excise duties are paid on goods produced or manufactured in a State and then passing into another State. In Section 95, customs duties are on goods passing into that State and not originally imported from beyond the limits of the Commonwealth. There is no explanation of the meaning of 'bounties'.

- The intentions behind these duties are important to States looking to broaden their taxation base. Given the Commonwealth, under Section 86, has legal power over customs, excise and bounties it could legislate to make the meaning of excise clearer.

- The Constitutional purpose of the Sections relating to trade was to create a customs union within the Commonwealth making the States dependant on the Commonwealth for any return of monies collected. In reality, it has restricted the taxing ability of the States and Territories. These Sections have been the subject of a number of High Court decisions. One result being an expansion of what excise means to further restrict the taxation powers of the States and Territories.

9. A Referendum is Required

Where a referendum is probably needed to make changes to the Constitution.

1. The Queen will receive monies from Consolidated Revenue to pay the Governor-General. Section 3.
2. The salary of the Governor-General is fixed during a term of office. Section 3.
3. Parliament to sit at least once a year. Section 6.
4. Each elector can only vote once in choosing a Senator. Section 8.
5. Making uniform laws for choosing Senators to represent States and dealing with any variation in numbers in the Senate. Sections 9 and 14.
6. House of Representatives members to be chosen by the people and in proportion to a State's population but with at least five members from each State. The Parliament can increase or decrease the number of House of Representatives members subject to the Constitution. Sections 24 and 27.
7. There will be twice as many House of Representative members as Senators. Section 24.
8. If State laws prohibit all persons of any race from voting in State lower house elections, these people will not be

counted to determine State representation in the Commonwealth House of Representative elections. Section 25.

9. Members of Parliament cannot be chosen or sit if they are disqualified under a number of conditions. For example: dual citizenship, treason allegations, certain prison sentences, bankruptcy and monetary interests in Government departments or businesses. A member's seat will become vacant if the member is disqualified. Sections 44 and 45.

10. Laws appropriating revenue for the ordinary annual service of Government and laws imposing taxation or dealing with customs and excise cannot deal with other issues. Sections 54 and 55.

11. The House of Representatives can resolve a deadlock with the Senate by way of a double dissolution election followed by a joint sitting of the Parliament if necessary. Section 57.

12. There will be a Federal Executive Council to advise the Governor-General. Sections 62 and 63.

13. Ministers of State must sit in the Parliament. Section 64.

14. The judicial power of the Commonwealth is vested in the High Court and other Federal Courts the Parliament creates. Section 71.

15. Revenues raised or received by the Executive Government of the Commonwealth go to a Consolidated Revenue Fund

to pay for Commonwealth expenditure and these appropriations are drawn by law. Sections 81, 82 and 83.

16. Public service officers transferred from a State to the Commonwealth employ should not be financially disadvantaged. Section 84.

17. The Commonwealth may acquire State property associated with the transfer of departments but with compensation. Section 85.

18. The Commonwealth has exclusive control over the collection and control of customs and excise and to grant bounties on the production or export of goods. Trade within the Commonwealth is to be free. Sections 86, 90, 92, 99 and 112.

19. The Commonwealth's power to make laws regarding trade and commerce extends to navigation and shipping and State railways. Section 98.

20. The Commonwealth can take over a State's public debts. Sections 105 and 105A.

21. The Commonwealth cannot curtail the rights of a State or resident to reasonable use of river water for conservation or irrigation. Section 100.

22. The Commonwealth cannot legislate to impinge on religious freedom. Section 116.

23. The Commonwealth will protect the States against invasion and if called upon by a State, against internal unrest. Section 119.

24. The Commonwealth can make laws regarding the State's responsibilities over persons accused or convicted of Commonwealth offences. Section 120.

25. The Commonwealth can admit or establish new States and make laws for the government of any territory surrendered by a State. Sections 121 and 122.

26. The limits of a State may be altered by the Commonwealth if the State and its electors agree. Section 123.

27. The Commonwealth Parliament can determine its location (in New South Wales). Section 125.

Comments

<u>Consolidated Revenue Fund</u>

- The Treasury of the Commonwealth, set out in Section 83 of the Constitution, is probably the same as the Consolidated Revenue Fund (CRF) established by Section 81. This Fund is composed of all monies collected by the Commonwealth (taxes, charges, loans, trust monies). The Constitution stipulates in Section 83 that money can only be taken from Treasury by law. This appropriation law must specify the purpose for which the money is required and the amount to be spent. This provides the Parliament with control over expenditure.

- The Constitution does not specify where the CRF is kept or how it is to be managed. The 'Financial Management and

Accountability Act, 1997' (replacing the' Audit Act, 1901'), provides a framework for dealing with and managing the money and property of the Commonwealth.

Taxation

- Sections in the Constitution relating to the raising of revenue cut across several chapters of the Constitution but the principle Sections as they apply to taxation are as follows.
- Section 51(ii) gives the Commonwealth the power to make taxation laws so long as they do not discriminate between States or parts of a State.
- Section 53 prohibits the Senate from originating laws appropriating revenue or imposing taxation.
- Section 55 states that proposed taxation laws may deal with one matter only.
- Section 114 prohibits a State from imposing a tax on Commonwealth property and vice versa.
- Section 90 gives the Commonwealth exclusive power to impose customs and excise duties.
- Section 96 allows the Commonwealth to provide financial assistance to States on its terms.
- Section 109 dictates that Commonwealth law prevails over State law.

The Constitution and the 1942 'Commonwealth Income Tax Act', where States gave over any ability to raise income tax to the Commonwealth in exchange for reimbursement, via

Grants ('Grants Income Tax Reimbursement Act, 1942'), has meant the Commonwealth can raise the most money while the States have considerable spending responsibilities (hospitals, schools, infrastructure). This has been termed vertical fiscal imbalance and allows the Commonwealth Government (principally the executive arm of the House of Representatives) to dictate policy to the States in return for financial grants.

<u>Religion</u>

- Section 116 of the Constitution prohibits the Commonwealth Government from;
- making laws to establish a religion,
- imposing any religious observance,
- preventing the free exercise of any religion, and,
- imposing any religious test as a qualification for Commonwealth office.

- The religious freedom granted by Section 116 is one of the few rights set out in the Constitution. However, this protections for religious freedom applies to the Commonwealth. Tasmania is the only State to provide for religious freedom in its Constitution.
- Human rights in Australia, such as freedom of religion, are protected legally and by common law. The 'Racial Discrimination Act, 1975', provides some protection against discrimination on the basis of religion if it can be shown that

a religious group has 'racial' links. The 'Workplace Relations and Other Legislation Amendment Act, 1966', includes the prohibition of discrimination on the grounds of religion. Under the 'Human Rights and Equal Opportunity Commission Act, 1986', the Commission can investigate violations of the right to freedom of religion and belief where the Commonwealth is at fault.

- A recent debate over same sex marriage with implications for religious ministers and wedding service providers, along with issues surrounding the wearing of dress associated with a religion has resulted in a review of religious freedom in Australia. The Federal Government commissioned the 'Ruddock Religious Freedom Review in 2017'. The report has been handed to the Commonwealth Government but not released publicly. There has been a suggestion for a Federal Religious Discrimination Act to achieve nationally consistent rules.

It is notable that the Constitution gives the Commonwealth Parliament (and the High Court) considerable lee way in altering and expanding the Constitution. This is in contrast to the forty four times the electors were asked to approve changes by means of a referendum. The electors only did so on eight occasions. Does this suggest a reluctance on the part of the public to grant the Commonwealth Government more power, uncertainty over the implications of any

change to the Constitution or simply, a view that a suggested change was not warranted?

10. The States

At the time of Federation, the States were self-governing entities and it was assumed they would carry on government under their own Constitutions at the same time as becoming united in the Commonwealth of Australia.

The Constitution sets out the position of the States as follows.

1. The States are to be represented by Senators chosen by their people. Section 7.
2. The Parliament of each State can make laws for the method of choosing their Parliamentarians, as long as the Commonwealth has not done so. Sections 9, 10, 30 and 31.
3. The Senate can operate even if a State does not provide Senators. Section 11.
4. A State Governor can issue writs for the election of Senators in that State. Section 12.
5. If a casual Senate vacancy occurs, the relevant State Parliament chooses a successor, from the same political party if possible. Section 15.
6. A State receives representation in the House of Representatives in proportion their population. Section 24.
7. If a State law prevents a person of any race from voting, these persons are not counted for the purpose of

determining representation in the House of Representatives. Section 25.

8. An adult person with the right to vote in a State election is able to vote at Commonwealth Parliamentary elections. Section 41.

9. The Constitution gives the Commonwealth the power to legislate over a number of areas (the responsibilities given to the States are rarely mentioned). Section 51.

10. The Commonwealth cannot discriminate between States in matters of taxation or legislate over State banks or insurance that is within a State's borders. Section 51.

11. The Commonwealth Parliament has the power to make laws over trade and commerce amongst the States that extends to railways, navigation and shipping which are State property (no mention of road or air). Sections 51(i) and 98.

12. The Federal Government has control over the civil and criminal process and the judgements of State courts. Section 51(xxiv).

13. The acquisition of property on just terms from the State or persons where the Commonwealth has power to make laws. Section 51(xxxi).

14. The acquisition, construction or extension of State railways with the State's consent. Sections 51(xxxiii) and 51(xxxiv).

15. Industrial disputes that go beyond a State's boundaries. Section 51(xxxv).

16. The Commonwealth Parliament has the power to make laws with the agreement or behest of the States. Sections 51(xxxvii) and 51(xxxviii).

17. The Governor-General receives powers similar to a Colonial (State) Governor in respect of matters which pass to the Commonwealth from a Colony (State). Section 70.

18. The High Court can hear appeals from the Supreme Court of a State and has jurisdiction over matters 'between States, or between residents of different States, or between a State and a resident of another State (or any subject that is also covered by State law)'. Sections 73, 75 and 76.

19. The Commonwealth Parliament can make laws giving any State Court federal jurisdiction and conferring rights to proceed against the Commonwealth or a State. Sections 77 and 78.

20. Infringements against the Commonwealth are to be tried in the State where the offence occurred. Trial is by jury, on indictment (charged as a serious crime). Section 80.

21. When a public service department is transferred to the Commonwealth from a State, officers (and any connected departmental property), comes under the jurisdiction of the Executive Government of the Commonwealth. Compensation can be negotiated. Sections 84 and 85.

22. At Federation, the control of customs, excise and bounties passed from the States to the Commonwealth. Of the net revenue collected, three quarters was to go to the States

(although it seems the Commonwealth can change this arrangement). Sections 86, 87, 89, 90 and 94.

23. The States can place a bounty on gold, silver or other minerals, although the Commonwealth Parliament would need to sanction any State involvement in bounties on the production or export of goods. Section 91.

24. Trade and commerce among the States is to be free. Section 92.

25. The States can receive financial assistance from the Commonwealth on its terms. Section 96.

26. The Federal Parliament has a responsibility to ensure revenue raising across the Commonwealth is reviewed and audited. Section 97.

27. The Commonwealth cannot make laws which discriminate between States in regard to trade and commerce regulation. Section 99.

28. States and their residents have rights to a reasonable use of rivers for conservation or irrigation which cannot be curtailed by Commonwealth legislation. Section 100.

29. The Commonwealth can stop any State giving preferences or discriminating in respect of railways. Any dispute over rates charged on the railways is to be resolved by the Interstate Commission. Sections 102 and 104.

30. The Commonwealth Parliament can take over the public debts of States. Sections 105 and 105A.

31. A State's constitution, laws and the powers of their Parliaments could continue after Federation although subject to the Commonwealth Constitution. Sections 106, 107 and 108.

32. If a State law is inconsistent with a Commonwealth law, the later prevails. Section 109.

33. States can surrender territory to the Commonwealth which can make laws for the governing of surrendered territory. With the permission of electors and a State, the Commonwealth can change State boundaries. Sections 111, 122, 123 and 124.

34. The States can make laws and charge fees for inspecting the import and export of goods (although the Commonwealth can annul these laws). Section 112.

35. The States have control over laws dealing with fermented, distilled or other intoxicating liquids that enter or are produced in a State. Section 113.

36. The Commonwealth and the States cannot tax each other's property. Section 114.

37. A State cannot raise a naval or military force without permission from the Commonwealth. The Commonwealth is required to protect States against internal or external threats. Sections 114 and 119.

38. A State is not allowed to coin money but can use gold and silver coins to pay debts. Section 115.

39. State residents have the same rights in all other States. Section 117.

40. 'Full faith and credit shall be given, throughout the Commonwealth, to the laws, the public Acts and records, and the judicial proceedings of every State' (no penalties are prescribed). Section 118.

41. The State is responsible for the detention and punishment of accused and convicted persons who have offended against the Commonwealth. The Commonwealth can legislate to give effect to this requirement. Section 120.

42. The seat of Commonwealth Government will be in the State of New South Wales. Section 125.

43. A referendum to decide on a proposed law to alter the Constitution must be passed not only by a majority of all electors but by a majority of States and a majority of these State's electors. Section 128.

Comments: How have States Fared under the Commonwealth Constitution?

<u>State Sovereignty</u>

- Between 1865 and 1986 the States were under the 'Colonial Laws Validity Act, 1865'. The States were regarded as self-governing dependencies of the British Government. The 'Australia Acts, 1986', passed by the Australian Commonwealth and the British Parliament, removed all colonial restrictions on State Parliaments. State Governors were independent of the Commonwealth, although the Commonwealth Constitution gave a Governor two roles on behalf of the Commonwealth. Under Section 12, a State Governor can issue writs for the election of State Senators and traditionally, a senior State Governor can stand-in for the Governor-General if necessary.

Diminishing Powers of the States

- Sections 106 and 107 of the Commonwealth Constitution preserved the State's constitutions and legislative powers after Federation. However, there are numerous Sections of the Commonwealth Constitution that allow for the expansion of the executive power of the Federal Government.
- The States' previous collection and control of bounties, customs and excise duties passed to the Commonwealth.
- The Commonwealth Parliament has the power to make laws concerning corporations under the 'Corporations Act 2001', giving them control over much of Australian business. This was an expansion of Section 51(xx) because the States referred their powers over the incorporation process to the Commonwealth as permitted by Section 51(xxxvii).
- Under Section 51(xxxv), the Commonwealth could enact legislation in industrial relations where disputes extended beyond State borders. The States referred their industrial

relations powers to national workplace relations under the Fair Work Acts.

- In Section 51(vi), the Commonwealth is given defence power but not internal security. The States referred some power to the Commonwealth under the 'Criminal Code Amendment (Terrorism) Act 2003'.

- The Federal Parliament was given the power to make laws with respect to trade and commerce.

- The States relinquished their rights to collect income tax in 1942 and under the 'Grants (Income Tax Reimbursement) Act, 1942', received money from the Commonwealth.

- With control over external affairs, the Commonwealth has been able to use international agreements like the 'Human Rights Covenants' to legislate broadly.

- The Commonwealth management of a number of social services gives it wide ranging powers.

- There has been a reduction in the judicial power of the States with the establishment of the Family Court in 1976 and the Federal Court in 1976 which can hear claims arising out of State law.

- The use of catch-all Sections of the Commonwealth Constitution such as Sections 51(xxxix) and 52(iii) where the Federal Parliament is provided with power over 'other matters' and 'matters incidental' in the Constitution can permit intrusion into State affairs.

- Local councils are under the remit of State (and Northern Territory) Governments. Through the 'Roads to Recovery Program' and the 'Regional and Local Community Infrastructure Program' the Commonwealth has provided direct funding to local governments. This can be seen as an attack on State sovereignty.

- The Commonwealth has become a major collector of revenue and through conditional grants to the States, gained some control over State policies. This has led to confusion on the part of the public about where responsibilities lie and who is accountable when problems occur. Vertical Fiscal Imbalance refers to a misalignment between revenue collected by a State or Territory and its economic needs to service responsibilities. This situation seems likely to remain as States have shown a reluctance to raise their own income tax and it does allow the Commonwealth Government a means to equalise revenue across the States and Territories. While the Commonwealth dominates the field of taxation, it shifts the balance of power to the Federal Parliament. There have been calls for the Commonwealth to take over the funding (but not the servicing) of public hospitals to try and reduce the fiscal imbalance and for the States and Territories to be given a share of the income tax collected by the Commonwealth.

<u>Lines of Responsibility between the States and the Commonwealth</u>

- The Australian Constitution lists, in Section 51, some forty areas over which the Federal Parliament can legislate. The States' powers are not listed. In essence, Federal expenditure was aimed at defence, external affairs, national infrastructure and social welfare with the States concentrating on education, health and local infrastructure. The expansion of Australia, the superior financial situation of the Commonwealth and broad interpretations of the Constitution by the High Court, has resulted in blurred lines of responsibility between the Commonwealth and the States. There is policy duplication, blame shifting and high costs associated with complying with varying regulations in different jurisdictions.

  - Safe Work Australia develops national policy to improve workers' health and safety and compensation arrangements in the country but cautions employers that they must meet the acts and regulations in a particular State or Territory.

  - The 'Environmental Protection and Biodiversity and Conservation (EPBC) Act, 1999', covers the assessment and approval process of national and cultural concerns. However, each business type needs to understand which Federal, State, Territory or local government law applies to its application and any approval under the 1999 Act, would be in addition to any State, Territory or local government law.

- This overlap in business regulation is repeated in building product manufacture requirements, training and licensing requirements for workers, mining regulations, and food standards to name a few areas.

- The Constitution does not set out rules to manage Commonwealth-State relations or provide for any back up structures to facilitate those relations. To fill this gap, Co-operative Federalism, a term used for the working relationships between the Commonwealth and the States, has evolved. This has no explicit constitutional authority but operates through a multitude of intergovernmental arrangements. The arrangements record commitments made by the Council of Australian Governments (COAG) and may lead to State or Commonwealth legislation.

- COAG consists of The Prime Minister, the Premiers and Chief Ministers and the President of the Australian Local Government Association. Some examples of arrangements are;

- the 'Intergovernmental Agreement Implementation (GST) Act, 2000',

- the 2012 Intergovernmental Agreement on the National Disability Insurance Scheme Launch,

- the 2009 Intergovernmental Agreement on Federal Financial Relations, and,

- the 2017 agreement on implementing water reform in the Murray Darling Basin.

The COAG website lists about forty Intergovernmental Agreements but there is likely to be many more not set out there. These agreements attempt to provide a national approach to policy areas so there is a better definition of roles between the Commonwealth, the States and Territories and Local Government. However, they do not pretend to interpret the Constitution as to roles and responsibilities but are more like a 'political compact' to make national arrangements as Australia has progressed since Federation.

- From 2017, the Productivity Commission will report on the performance of these agreements. This Commission is an Australian Government independent authority set up by an Act in 1998 with a remit to provide independent advice and information to the Government.
- The public has little opportunity to understand which arm of government is funding and delivering services. In an effort to make the best of the situation delivered in the Constitution, the States, Territories and the Commonwealth have come to agreements in an effort to improve funding transparency. The 'Intergovernmental Agreement on Federal Financial Relations, 2009', is an agreement to continue GST grants to States and Territories based on fiscal equalisation

and to work collaboratively to simplify the process of Specific Purpose Payments and other grants to the States and Territories (as per Section 96 of the Constitution). The 'COAG reform Fund Act, 2008', established the COAG reform fund as a special account under the Consolidated Revenue Fund to provide more transparency in the grant process. These are voluntary agreements and not part of the current Constitution.

- It would be difficult to try and unwind the status quo and definitively divide responsibilities between the States, Territories, Local Government and the Commonwealth. The Constitution is no longer the major determinant of the roles and responsibilities of the Commonwealth, the States and Territories and local government. Section 51 is an historical guide but the Constitution needs to introduce an established and ongoing body to determine areas of national importance, a role for the Commonwealth, and the service responsibilities of the States, Territories and local governments. This body would identify areas of unnecessary duplication and align financing and policy development.

- In a Federation, with changing social, technological and economic conditions, flexibility and the ability to evolve is essential. The Constitution could give a more substantial role to COAG with supporting administration and use the guiding principles outlined after the Premiers' and Chief Ministers' Conference in 1991. These are reproduced below.

(i) Australian nation principle: all governments in Australia recognise the social, political and economic imperative of nationhood and will work co-operatively to ensure that national issues are resolved in the interests of Australia as a whole.

(ii) Subsidiary principle: responsibility for regulation and for allocation of public goods should be devolved to the maximum extent possible consistent with the national interest, so that government is accessible and accountable to those affected by its decisions.

(iii) Structural efficiency principle: increased competitiveness and flexibility in the Australian economy requires structural reform in the public sector to complement private sector reform. Inefficient Commonwealth-State division of functions can no longer be tolerated.

(iv) Accountability principle: the structure of intergovernmental arrangements should promote democratic accountability and the transparency of government to the electorate.

All governments would include local government and accountability would include a role for Parliamentary Committees to examine draft intergovernmental agreements and tied grants for greater transparency and accountability and reporting to Parliament. All intergovernmental agreements should be easily available to the public.

<u>The Poor Wording of the Constitution in Relation to Chapter V:
The States</u>

Chapter V of the Constitution which deals with the States provides many examples of why the Constitution needs to be rewritten. This Chapter;

- does not indicate how a Colony becomes a State despite using the terms interchangeably (vagueness),
- implies that the Commonwealth can withdraw powers from the States whilst also stating that State/Colony laws in force at Federation will remain (confusion),
- indicates the States have control over the sale and storage of alcoholic liquids without mentioning excise (inconsistency),
- gives State residents rights as subjects of the queen (historical),
- allows residents to be subject to a disability or discrimination as long as they are treated equally across States (perverse), and,
- states that 'full faith and credit be given to the laws, the public Acts and records, and the judicial proceedings of any State' (incomprehensible).

<u>The States Under a Commonwealth Republic</u>

- If the Commonwealth became a republic, it would be preferable for the States to amend their constitutions to accommodate the change in status. Prior to the 1999 referendum, to determine if Australia should become a republic, an agreement was reached with the States to change their constitutions to align with the Commonwealth.

11. The Territories

1. A State Parliament may surrender any part to the Commonwealth which will come under Commonwealth jurisdiction. Sections 111, 122, 123 and 124.
2. Any referendum on the Commonwealth constitution will be submitted to each State and Territory. Section 128.

<u>How Does a Territory Differer from a State?</u>

- The 'Commonwealth of Australia Act, 1900 (UK)', which contains the Australian Constitution in part 9, defines the meaning of a State in part 6 as:

"The Commonwealth" shall mean the Commonwealth of Australia as established under this Act. "The States" shall mean such of the colonies of New South Wales, New Zealand, Queensland, Tasmania, Victoria, Western Australia and South Australia, including the Northern Territory of South Australia, as for the time being are parts of the Commonwealth, and such colonies or territories may be admitted into or established by the Commonwealth as States; and each such parts of the Commonwealth shall be called "a State". "Original State" shall mean such States as are parts of the Commonwealth at its establishment.

Presumably, a Territory is anything other than a State.

<u>How Many Territories Does the Commonwealth Parliament Administer?</u>

- There are ten Australian Territories. The Northern Territory and the Australian Capital Territory are self-governing and represented in the Commonwealth Parliament. Norfolk Island has some measure of autonomy with an elected council. The remaining seven territories are administered by various departments in the Federal Government. They are the Australian Antarctic Territory, Ashmore and Cartier Islands, Christmas Island, Cocos (Keeling) Island, Coral Sea Islands, Jervis Bay Territory and the Territory of Heard Island and the McDonald Islands.

12. The Judicature

1. There will be a Federal Supreme Court called the High Court of Australia plus other federal courts created by the Commonwealth. Section 71.

2. The High Court will consist of a Chief Justice and at least two other Justices. The Commonwealth can increase the number of Justices and can fix their renumeration. It can also determine the number of judges in other federal courts. Sections 71, 72 and 79.

3. Justices of the High Court are appointed and removed by the Governor-General in Council and must retire by age seventy. Section 72.

4. The Commonwealth Government can determine the jurisdiction of the High Court and this power seems to extend to other Federal Courts and give federal jurisdiction to State Courts. The judgement of the High Court is final. Sections 73 and 77.

5. The High Court can hear some cases without them having to first go to a lower court. These cases are: matters arising under any treaty; affecting consuls; if the Commonwealth is being sued; between States or residents of different States and issuing actions against a Commonwealth officer. The Parliament can include other cases that involve the interpretation of the Constitution, issues arising from

Parliamentary laws, maritime matters and some State laws. Sections 75 and 76.

6. The Parliament may make laws conferring rights to proceed against the Commonwealth or a State in respect of matters within the limits of the judicial power. Section 78.

Comments

The Court System and Commonwealth Power

* Section 71 sets up the High Court of Australia and allows the Commonwealth to create other Federal Courts. It also gives the Commonwealth the power to, 'invest Federal jurisdiction in other courts'. This potentially allows the Federal Parliament to take over State Courts. Section 73 allows the High Court jurisdiction over areas, 'the Parliament prescribes' and Section 75 enables the Parliament to extend to the High Court access to 'original jurisdiction' or the ability to hear cases not originating in a lower court.

Appointment of Justices

* In practice, the justices of the High Court are appointed by the executive government. The Constitution does not indicate the process by which this happens (other than to say appointments are made by the Governor-General) or the desirable qualifications of appointees. There is a need for the Commonwealth Government to explain a particular

appointment and the qualities of the appointee. Otherwise, if the process is completed in secret, there is the suggestions that ideology and or politics are involved.

<u>Obscure Terms and Wording</u>

Chapter III of the Constitution which deals with the Judicature would defy the average citizen's attempts to understand the meaning of some terms and phrase. For example: 'a writ of Mandamus'; 'original jurisdiction'; 'Her Majesty in Council' and the bewildering last paragraph in Section 72 which deals with judges' appointments, tenure and renumeration.

'A reference in this section to the appointment of a Justice of the High Court or of a court created by the Parliament shall be read as including a reference to the appointment of a person who holds office as a Justice of the High Court or of a court created by the Parliament to another office of Justice of the same court having a different status or designation'.

13. Redundant Sections of the Constitution

The Constitution is showing its age. Not only has Commonwealth legislation and High Court decisions reshaped the Constitution but passages that are no longer relevant emphasise the need for an upgrade.

- The following Sections and parts thereof could be removed.
    - Section 5 where the Constitution refers to the first session of the Commonwealth Parliament.
    - Section 15 which deals with Senate positions before the commencement of the 'Constitution Alteration (Senate Casual Vacancies) Act, 1977'.
    - Section 26 concerns the number of representatives in the first Parliament.
    - References to appeals to the Queen in Council (Privy Council). Sections 73 and 74.
    - Transfer of State departments to the Commonwealth on its establishment. Section 69.
    - Money the Governor-General can appropriate until one month after the first meeting of the Commonwealth Parliament. Section 83.
    - Section 89 deals with payments to the States before uniform duties.

- Section 90 that allows States to impose bounties that were lawful before 1898 (do any still exist?).
- Section 94 deals with the payment of any surplus revenue the Commonwealth collected five years after the imposition of uniform customs duties. In 1908, a Surplus Revenue Act of the Commonwealth Parliament allowed the Commonwealth to pay surplus revenue into trust accounts (to finance pensions). This made Section 94 redundant.
- Section 95 concerns Western Australian customs duties for the first five years of the Commonwealth.
- Sections 101, 103 and 104 concern the Inter-State Commission which no longer exists.

14. Altering the Current Constitution

Section 128 of the Constitution sets out the means by which the Constitution can be changed by the Australian electors. There has not been a great success rate with only nine of forty four proposals being successful.

<u>How Should a Referendum be put to the Electors?</u>

- The Australian Electoral Commission states that in a referendum, 'voters have to write either 'Yes' or 'No' in the box opposite each question on the ballot paper'. However, according to Section 128, a proposed change to the Constitution must start as a bill or proposed law (not a question). This bill has to pass the Parliament before it can be voted on by electors in a referendum.
- Mr Shorten, the leader of the opposition in the Federal Parliament in 2018, has promised a referendum on Australia becoming a republic by putting this question to voters, 'Do you support an Australian Republic with an Australian head of state?' A question to be answered 'Yes' or 'No'. Is this a lawful proposal in its present form?
- In 1977, Australian voters were asked the following question in relation to the retirement age of judges of the High Court and other federal courts', 'It is proposed to alter the Constitution so as to provide for retiring ages for judges of

federal courts'. This referendum passed without voters knowing what the proposed retirement age would be. Furthermore, the the resulting Act, 'Constitution Alterations (Retirement of Judges), 1977', stipulated that current judges were not affected by the mandated 70 years retirement rule, and the Parliament could vary or amend the 1977 law. Did the voters anticipate these outcomes when they voted on the question above?

- A 1967 referendum asked, 'Do you approve the proposed law for the alteration of the Constitution entitled, 'An Act to alter the Constitution so as to omit certain words relating to the People of the Aboriginal race in any state so that Aborigines are to be counted in reckoning the population'. This Act was designed to remove the words; 'other than the aboriginal race in any state' from the original section 51(xxvi) of the Constitution. In this case the subsequent Act, 'Constitutional Alteration (Aboriginals) 1967', was true to the referendum question.

15. Creating a New Constitution

In a democracy, a constitution is one way people gain some control over their government. Australian citizens deserve a constitution that has an impact on their lives and provides a fix for a perceived problem or makes their lives better. A constitution is a national set of rules that should tell Australians how they are governed as well as the standards expected of politicians, their staff and the public service.

It would be best if States made their constitutions fit a Commonwealth Republic at the time it is constituted. Before the 1999 referendum on the republic, all States and the Commonwealth reached an agreement that if the referendum carried, all State Governments would propose amendments to their State constitutions to bring them into line with a revised Commonwealth constitution.

A new constitution needs to be out of the hands of the politicians (and as clear as possible to reduce litigation). One way of updating the Commonwealth Constitution is to convene a Convention of delegates elected by the people. A draft constitution would be sent for political comment. The draft would then need to be legislated and passed by both House of the Commonwealth Parliament before Australian electors would vote in a referendum. This is a method followed by Iceland in recent times and there is a call to update the Irish Constitution via a peoples' convention. Professor George Williams (ABC, August, 2017) has suggested a Constitution Commission to put proposals for change to the electorate.

It may be necessary, given the difficulty of persuading politicians to initiate a reform process, to go outside the current party system and form a new party with the remit to start the reform process. At the Adelaide Festival of Ideas in 2016, Barry Jones delivered the 20th Don Dunstan Oration on 'The Courage Party? Climbing out of the political abyss'. Jones was looking for a Party that would be ' a powerful agent for change and could transform the political agenda'. Present political debate was seen as infantile and narrow. Politicians as super cautious and afraid to tackle the great issues of our time. Instead of a 'Courage Party', Australia needs a 'Constitution Party' to manage a root and branch reform of a Constitution which is more than one hundred years old to bring the workings of government closer to the aspirations and needs of Australians. Is the Australian Constitution so great that it can't be updated after more than a century? It was after all, a transitional document to get the Federation up and running.

The 'Constitution Party' would not be composed of career politicians. Few voters belong to a political party and are sceptical of politicians from the major parties who are funded by the trade unions and big business. There is a need to attract independent people with a variety of skills who can focus on the needs and aspirations of the people who elected them. Citizens in each electorate should be encouraged to nominate potential members of Parliament willing to rewrite the blueprint for future governments, not vote slavishly for a candidate forced on them by current political parties.

No one person can construct a new constitution for the Commonwealth of Australia. This is a plea to update and make the document more comprehensible and reflective of how the Commonwealth Government operates. It is an opportunity for the people of Australia to exercise their sovereign right and decide how the fundamental law of the country will be written. The proposed constitution which follows is, of course, only a suggestion.

16. An Updated Australian Constitution

Preamble

We the people of the Federal Republic of Australia.

-Recognise the indigenous people as original custodians of the land, their unique culture, customs, traditions and languages.

-Believe that Australia belongs to all who live in it and the welfare of all peoples is based on principles of freedom, equality and justice.

-Value autonomy, minimal government intrusion, the dignity of work, our own income and strive for a world class health and education system.

-Provide this Constitution for the purpose of promoting good government for the welfare of present and future peoples.

A. The Commonwealth Parliament

1. The Commonwealth Parliament shall be formed when eligible citizens elect members to the House of Representatives and the Senate.

2. Groups of like-minded people can become a political party when registered and members are nominated for a Parliamentary seat.

3. The party or coalition of parties with a working majority in the House of Representatives will form the Commonwealth Government.

4. The leader of the majority party (or parties) in the House of Representatives becomes the Prime Minister.

5. There may be an opposition leader who has the support of the party (or parties) in a minority in the House of Representatives.

6. The Parliament shall sit at least once in every six months from gaining office.

7. The Parliament proposes legislation and if passed by both Houses, this legislation becomes law and will be published as such.

B. The Australian Public Service

1. There will be an Australian Public Service responsible for public administration, policy and service of departments and agencies of the Commonwealth Government. The operations of the public service will be governed by a publicly available Code of Conduct. This Code of Conduct will also apply to ministerial advisers.

2. If any department of a State public service is transferred to the Commonwealth, personnel will not lose any rights of

employment owing to them as State employees. The Commonwealth shall compensate the State for the value of any property passing to the Commonwealth.

C. The Prime Minister

1. The Prime Minister selects Ministers of State and Parliamentary Secretaries from the House of Representatives or the Senate and allocates portfolios of responsibility. These people form the Executive who administer the country using laws passed by the Parliament. The Prime Minister may dismiss members from these positions.

2. The Prime Minster is able to call, suspend or dissolve sessions of the House of Representatives.

3. The appointment and removal of public servants is vested in the Prime Minister or by the Prime Minister's authority to another person.

4. The Prime Minister is Commander-in-Chief of Australia's armed forces. Only Parliament can deploy armed forces unless Australia is subject to direct attack and the decision then rests with the Prime Minister.

D. The Judiciary

1. There will be an independent judiciary to interpret and apply the law without interference from the Parliament or the Executive.

2. The Judiciary ensures laws and the administration of government is within the powers outlined by this Constitution.

3. There will be a High Court of Australia that can hear final appeals in civil and criminal matters from all Australian courts. This Court has jurisdiction on any matter arising under the Constitution or involving its interpretation or arising under any laws made by Parliament.

4. The High Court will consist of a Chief Justice and other Justices as decided by the Commonwealth Parliament.

5. The High Court will have the power to decide which appeal cases it will consider.

6. The High Court can hear cases for the first time (original jurisdiction) in all matters;

(i) arising under any treaty,

(ii) affecting consuls or other representatives of other countries,

(iii) in which the Commonwealth, or a person suing or being sued on behalf of the Commonwealth is a party,

(iv) between State or Territories, or between residents of different States or Territories, or between a State or Territory and a resident of another State or Territory, and,

(v) when a Commonwealth Officer has failed to perform an enforceable legal duty (mandamus), has exceeded their powers (prohibition) or has otherwise acted unlawfully (injunction).

7. The Commonwealth Parliament may create subordinate federal courts with jurisdiction over laws made by the Parliament.

8. The appointment, dismissal and retirement of High Court Judges.

(i) When a vacancy occurs in the High Court, each State Attorney General and the Commonwealth Attorney General will suggest candidates. The successful candidate will be selected by the Prime Minister who will provide public reasons for a candidate's successful appointment.

(ii) The Parliament may decide on a retirement age for judges.

(iii) Judges can only be removed on the grounds of misbehaviour or incapacity by a vote of the Parliament.

(iv) Judges may resign in writing to the Prime Minister.

E. Commonwealth Parliamentary Elections

1. The following citizens are eligible to vote;

(i) reached the age of 18 years,

(ii) an Australian citizen, and,

(iii) of sound mind and able to understand the election process.

2. The following citizens are not eligible to vote;

(i) people serving a prison sentence of more than 3 years, and,

(ii) a person convicted (and not pardoned) of treason or treachery.

3. Voting by eligible citizens is compulsory, by secret ballot and with one vote per person.

4. The Parliament will enact laws to establish an independent Electoral Commission to manage electoral representation, the registration of political parties and the process and procedures of a Commonwealth election, including procedures to resolve a dispute in election processes or results and the timing of writs and first session of a new Parliament.

5. Each State will be allocated a number of seats in the House of Representatives based on a State's population relative to the population of the Commonwealth of Australia.

6. A State will be divided into single member electorates with approximately the same population.

7. State electoral boundaries may be redrawn to take account of population changes and this review of boundaries must take place at least every 8 years.

8. The Northern Territory and the Australian Capital Territory will have two members each in the House of Representatives.

9. Elections for the House of Representatives will be by a preferential voting system.

10. There will be twice the number of members in the House of Representatives as in the Senate.

11. There must be at least five members from each State in the House of Representatives. The Parliament can alter the number of members of the Parliament subject to this proviso.

12. Each State will have an equal number of Senators. The Northern Territory and the Australian Capital Territory will have two Senators each.

13. Senate election results will be determined by proportional representation and a State is considered as one electorate.

F. Qualifications of Members of Parliament

1. To nominate for a seat in the Commonwealth Parliament a candidate must be;

(i) an Australian citizen domiciled in an Australian State or Territory for at least 3 years,

(ii) an elector who is over 25 years of age and entitled to vote, or a person qualified to become an elector

(iii) free of any involvements which might constitute a material conflict of interest between their government office and private interests,

(iv) able to demonstrate at least five years in employ that does not involve being a member of an Australian Parliament or employment by a current or serving Commonwealth, State or Territorial politician, and,

(v) willing to remain true to electors and not able to change party affiliation after being elected to a seat.

2. The following persons who subsequently become a member of Parliament will be deemed to be no longer employed or to hold office on the day they are sworn into Parliament;

(i) a judge or holds any other judicial office,

(ii) a member or employee of the Commonwealth, State or Territorial public service,

(iii) a member of the Defence Force, and,

(iv) a member of any other Australian Parliament or legislature.

3.   Penalties for sitting as a member when disqualified.

(i) The Parliament may decide if any pecuniary penalties are payable to the Commonwealth by a member of Parliament who is disqualified.

(ii) The House in which the question arises should determine any question respecting the qualifications of a member of the House.

(iii) An elector in the electorate of the person whose qualification or membership is in question is able to apply to the High Court for a judgement. Such a judgement has precedence over any determination of the respective House of the Parliament.

(iv) If a member is judged to be disqualified, the member's seat will be declared vacant.

G. Renumeration of Members of Parliament, Judges, a President and Senior Public Servants.

1. The Parliament will establish an independent Renumeration Tribunal to determine the renumeration and allowances of current and eligible former members of Parliament. Payment and allowances to Commonwealth

Court judges, a President and senior public servants shall also be determined by this Tribunal. These determinations will be published.

H. Oath or Affirmation of Allegiance to the Commonwealth of Australia

1. Members and Ministers of a new Commonwealth Parliament will take the oath, '*I solemnly and sincerely swear (or affirm) and declare that I will well and truly serve the Commonwealth of Australia*' in front of the Speaker of the House of Representatives or the President of the Senate.

I. The Operation of the House of Representatives

1. The House of Representatives, as its first task in a new Parliament, will elect a Speaker (and a Deputy Speaker) who swears in new members, accepts any resignations, oversees the administration of the House of Representatives and ensures members obey the rules of the House and follow the correct procedures. The Speaker may be removed by a vote of the House or can resign in writing to the Prime Minister.

2. The House of Representatives will make rules and orders about the way in which its powers, privileges and immunities may be exercised and upheld and the order and

conduct of its business and proceedings. These should be documented and published.

3. Any proposed legislation relating to taxation, customs and excise duties or the appropriation of revenue for the annual services of Government shall deal only with such tax, duties or appropriation.

4. Any appropriation of revenue requested by the House of Representatives must be passed by both Houses of Parliament.

5. In each financial year of a term of Government, the Treasurer will report on revenue spent in the areas of defence, education, health, public sector employ, social services and other welfare, State and Territory expenditure as well as monies to pay down debt. This will be published in a form easily interpreted by voters.

6. A member of the House of Representatives may resign in writing to the Speaker.

7. A vacancy in the House of Representatives between elections will be notified to the Electoral Commission by the Speaker and a by-election called. The Prime Minister may waive the by-election if a set-term general election is less than three months away.

8. Both Houses of the Parliament will be elected for a fixed term of 4 years. If the Prime Minister dissolves the House of Representative before this time both Houses will go to an election.

J. The Operation of the Senate

1. The Senate, as a first task in a new Parliament, will elect a President (and Deputy) who swears in new Senators, accepts any resignations, chairs meetings of the Senate, ensures members follow Senate rules and has overall responsibility for the administration of the Senate. The President may be removed by a vote of the House or can resign in writing to the Prime Minister.

2. A member of the Senate may resign in writing to the President of the Senate who will inform the relevant State Government.

3. A vacancy in the Senate between elections will be filled by the relevant State Parliament after notification by the Senate President. If the previous Senator was a member of a political party, the replacement Senator shall come from the same party if possible. The State may choose not to replace a Senator but this will not stop the business of the Senate.

4. No member of Parliament can simultaneously hold a seat in the House of Representatives and the Senate.

5. The President of the Senate and the Speaker of the House of Representatives will have joint responsibility for the provision of services to the Parliament.

6. The Senate will make rules and orders about the way in which its powers, privileges and immunities may be exercised and upheld and the order and conduct of its

business and proceedings. These should be documented and published.

7. The role of the Senate will be to review legislation initiated in the House of Representatives. Particular attention should be paid to State and Territory implications in proposed legislation.

8. The Senate has equal legislative powers with the House of Representatives except it cannot initiate or amend any laws relating to the appropriation of revenue or imposing of taxation. The Senate can refuse to pass such laws which can be returned to the House of Representatives with suggestions for amendment. However, the Senate can initiate legislation for the imposition or appropriation of fines or other pecuniary penalties, or for the demand or payment or appropriation of fees for licences, or fees for service under the proposed law.

9. If the Senate rejects or fails to pass, within thirty days of its transmission, a Bill it cannot amend, the Bill shall become law.

10. Voting on proposed legislation in the Senate shall be by secret ballot.

11. Each State will have an equal number of Senators. The Northern Territory and the Australian Capital Territory will have two Senators each.

K. Deadlock between Commonwealth Houses of Parliament

1. If a piece of proposed legislation, initiated in the House of Representatives, is not passed by the Senate after three months, the Prime Minister may call a joint sitting of the Parliament and if two thirds of members pass the legislation, it will become law.

L. Policy Implementation and Evaluation

1. All proposed policies and programmes set before the Executive of the Commonwealth Government should have a well documented implementation plan that is publicly available.
2. All Commonwealth Government funded programmes with a budget in excess of $10 million should be evaluated to determine if goals were achieved and value for money was delivered. Such programmes should be resourced for a finite time. Any continuation would be contingent on the outcome of the evaluation.
3. An office shall be established by the Commonwealth Parliament to examine all new laws to determine if they are internally consistent and don't negate aspects of other laws.

M. Integrity in the Commonwealth Government

1. There will be;

(i) a standing Independent Commission Against Corruption with educational, research and policy functions,

(ii) an Ombudsman to investigate complaints against a Government department or agency,   (iii) an Auditor-General to oversee the proper use and management of public moneys and property,

(iv) legislated protection for whistleblowers,

(v) an Office of Information Commissioner to oversee and review decisions made under a Freedom of Information Act and to make government information readily available to the public,

(vi) a legislated code of conduct for members of Parliament and their staff designed and regularly reviewed by public input, and,

(vii) an independent body will be established to monitor a register of lobbyists. There will be a legislated code of conduct with penalties for infringement of the code and the register must record any roles in corporations or State and Commonwealth Governments held by a lobbyist in the past five years.

2. The Parliament will provide for the following.

(i) Public funding of political parties and independents for election campaigns.

(ii) Publicly available information on contracts with the private sector.

(iii) A Parliamentary integrity adviser to educate members of Parliament and their staff on integrity matters and to register member's pecuniary interests.

3. The Parliament will ban the following.

(i) Paid access to members of Parliament or their staff.

(ii) Members of Parliament accepting post-parliamentary employment in, or for the Commonwealth Government in an any area of responsibility held in the life of the previous government.

N. Truth in Government

1. There will be;

(i) a Parliamentary Budget Office to provide costings on policy proposals, report on the fiscal impact of election commitments and provide public information and education on budget matters,

(ii) an Audit Office to provide Parliament with an independent assurance about public sector financial reporting, administration and accountability, and,

(iii) support for public broadcasting to ensure independent, accurate and impartial information is available to citizens.

O. Distribution of Legislative Power and Responsibility

1. As a general principle, legislative power will be at the level of government best able to exercise it.

2. The Commonwealth Parliament will work towards allowing more untied grants to the States and Territories and increase the financial independence of the States and Territories.

3. Legislative powers vested in the Commonwealth Parliament (the States and Territories are able to legislate in these areas but Commonwealth law will take precedence over State and Territory law should a dispute arise) are as follows.

(i) Anti-terrorism.

(ii) Astronomical and meteorological observations.

(iii) Banking other than State banking.

(iv) Bankruptcy and insolvency.

(v) Borrowing money on the public credit of the Commonwealth.

(vi) Bounties (on the production or export of goods).

(vii) Census and statistics.

(viii) Cities.

(ix) Copyrights, patents of inventions and designs, trade marks.

(x) Corporations.

(xi) Currency, coinage, paper money and other legal tender such as bills of exchange and promissory notes.

(xii) Customs duties (a tax imposed on goods entering or leaving Australia).

(xiii) Defence.

(xiv) Emigration and immigration.

(xv) Excise duties (a tax on a commodity at any point in the distribution before it meets the consumer).

(xvi) External affairs including relations with the islands of the Pacific.

(xvii) Federal police.

(xviii) Fisheries in Australian waters from three nautical miles offshore to the limit of Australia's Exclusive Economic Zone.

(xix) Foreign policy.

(xx) Foreign corporations and trading or financial corporations formed in the Commonwealth.

(xxi) Health.

(xxii) Higher education, University and technical training.

(xxiii) Indigenous Australians- laws for the advancement of these peoples

(xxiv) Industrial relations.

(xxv) Insurance other than State insurance.

(xxvi) Invalid and seniors pensions.

(xxvii) Lighthouses, lightships, beacons and buoys.

(xxviii) Marriage, divorce and matrimonial causes, parental and children's rights and the custody and guardianship of children

(xxix) Media.

(xxx) National disasters.

(xxxi) Naturalisations and aliens.

(xxxii) Population, immigration and emigration.

(xxxiii) Postal services, telegraphic, telephonic, internet and like services.

(xxxiv) Professional and trade qualifications.

(xxxv) Quarantine.

(xxxvi) Revenue raising.

(xxxvii) Science and information technology.

(xxxviii) Superannuation..

(xxxix) Trade and commerce with other countries and among the States and Territories.

(xl) Weights and measures.

(xli) Welfare such as; maternity allowances, widow allowances, aged pensions and care, family allowances, unemployment benefits, disability support, student benefits and pharmaceutical, medical and dental services.

5. Legislative power forbidden to the Commonwealth Parliament.

(i) No law or regulation of trade, commerce or revenue shall give preference to any State or Territory.

(ii) Impositions on religious freedom.

(iii) Retrospective legislation.

6. Legislative power exclusive to the Commonwealth Parliament.

(i) The location of the Commonwealth seat of Government.

(ii) Authority over the Commonwealth public service.

(iii) The command of defence forces is vested in the Commonwealth Parliament and Prime Minister.

(iv) Establishment of new states or territories.

6. Powers vested in the States.

(i) Agriculture.

(ii) Banking (State or Territory).

(iii) Child welfare, care and protection.

(iv) Bounties (royalties) on mining for gold, silver and other metals.

(v) Cities.

(vi) Courts (State or Territory).

(vii) Energy.

(viii) Fermented, distilled or other intoxicating liquids.

(ix) Fire and emergency services

(x) Fisheries in inshore waters

(xi) Gambling.

(xii) Health

(xiii) Indigenous affairs.

(xiv) Intra-state trade and commerce.

(xv) Industrial relations.

(xvi) Insurance (State or Territory).

(xvii) Internal water management.

(xviii) Land, mines and mining.

(xix) Local government.

(xx) Mining for gold, silver and other metals.

(xxi) Occupational health and safety.

(xxii) Police and prisons.

(xxiii) Pre-primary, Primary and Secondary education.

(xxiv) Public housing.

(xxv) Public transport.

(xxvi) Public works.

(xxvii) State rivers.

(xxviii) State banking and insurance.

(xxix) State fisheries and forests.

(xxx) State infrastructure.

(xxxi) State laws and courts.

(xxxii) State taxes.

(xxxiii) Tourism and leisure.

P. Co-operative Commonwealth State Relations

1. The States can refer matters to the Commonwealth Parliament to enact laws that extend to that State.

2. The Commonwealth Parliament can refer matters to a State so that State may incorporate the referred matter as law.

3. The Parliament of a State, with the consent of its people, may surrender any part of the State to the Commonwealth and this part will come under Commonwealth jurisdiction.

4. The Commonwealth may establish new States with the consent of existing States.

5. There will be a Council of Australian Governments, consisting of the State Premiers, the Territory Chief

Ministers and the President of the Australian Local Government Association to manage matters of national significance where co-ordinated action will benefit all Australians. This Council will meet at least twice a year and the agenda will be drawn with both State, Territory and Commonwealth input.

6. The Parliament may grant financial assistance to the States and Territories on terms and conditions that will reduce the fiscal imbalance and provide funding at the level of service delivery. There will be a Grants Commission to advise the Government on how revenue is distributed to place the States and Territories on a level playing field.

7. The Commonwealth Government, at the beginning of its term of office, will identify major challenges facing Australia and tell the public how it intends to work with the States and Territories to address them.

Q. Productivity

1. There will be a Productivity Commission to help the Commonwealth Government make policies that achieve a more productive and efficient economy.

2. There will be a statutory body with a mandate to accept government and community submissions so this body can prioritise and progress nationally significant infrastructure projects.

3. The Commonwealth Government will implement at least two long term policies which will transcend an election cycle.

4. Commonwealth labour market laws will be reviewed every five years to ensure they suit conditions of the prevailing workforce in terms of workers' rights and entitlements and the efficient running of business. Labour-hire contractors will be licensed.

R. Finance and Trade

1. All revenue raised or received by the Commonwealth Government must be paid into one Consolidated Revenue Fund. No money shall be drawn from this fund except under appropriation made by law and for a specific purpose.

2. The Commonwealth Parliament may grant financial assistance to a State or Territory.

3. The Parliament will enact laws to protect Australian consumers, investors and creditors. A Commission will be established to enforce and regulate these laws.

4. The Parliament will enact laws to promote competition, fair trading and consumer protection. A Commission will be established to ensure individuals and business comply with these laws.

5. The Treasurer will receive advice from an independent foreign investment review board on whether to approve

proposals by foreign interests wanting to invest in Australia.

6. Trade within the Commonwealth will be free.

7. The Commonwealth shall not by any law or regulation of trade, commerce, or revenue give preference to one State or Territory over another.

S. The People

1. A newly elected Commonwealth Government will involve a citizen jury, selected randomly from eligible voters, financed and resourced to consider and advise on at least one core piece of proposed legislation per year. This same jury will suggest one area for reform, by way of review, in the term of the Government.

2. The Commonwealth Government will enact privacy legislation to protect the personal information of identifiable individuals dealing with Commonwealth Government Agencies or businesses with an annual turnover of more than $3 million.

3. The people shall have the right to access information created by government.

4. The Commonwealth Parliament will consult with its citizens to develop and maintain a Charter of Human Rights. Particular attention will be paid to the effects of modern technologies on human rights.

5. The Commonwealth, in concert with the States, will establish programs to assist migrants to establish themselves in Australia.

T. The Non-Executive President

1. The President will be elected as follows.

(i) Each of the six States, plus the Northern Territory and the Australian Capital Territory, will nominate a person qualified and willing to be President. The candidates will then go to a first-past- the-post vote by citizens eligible to vote in a Commonwealth election.

2. To be eligible to serve as President the person;

(i) must be eligible to vote in Commonwealth elections,

(ii) have served Australia with distinction, and,

(iii) not be a member of any Australian Government.

3. The President's salary and allowances will be determined as for Commonwealth members of Parliament. The President cannot receive any other Commonwealth benefit whilst in office.

4. The President will have an official Canberra residence.

5. The President will be appointed for one five year term.

6. A President will take office within thirty days of being elected and make an oath before a joint sitting of Parliament and in front of the Chief Justice of the High Court:

'From this time forward (Under God) I swear I will be loyal to the Commonwealth of Australia and the Australian people in my role as President of the Commonwealth of Australia'

7.   The President may resign in writing to the Prime Minister.

8.   If the President is deemed unable to continue duties due to incapacity or misconduct, a joint sitting of Parliament, by a two-thirds majority, may effect a dismissal.

9.   The President will provide civic leadership by;

(i) being a patron of arts, culture and charitable organisations,

(ii) visiting local communities and hosting cultural events,

(iii) awarding honours to deserving citizens, and,

(iv) making speeches that reflect the shared values and aspirations of Australians.

10. The President will have a role in promoting the image and reputation of Australia in other countries at the request of the Prime Minister by;

(i) accrediting and receiving ambassadors and other dignitaries, and,

(ii) representing Australia overseas.

U. Altering the Constitution

1.   Proposed legislation for the amendment of the Constitution must set out the exact wording of the proposed law that will be written into the Constitution and be passed by the House of Representatives and the Senate.

2. If the Government chooses, this legislation can be presented to the voting public as a referendum.

3. The proposed legislation becomes law if approved by a majority of voting Australians and wins a majority in a majority of States.

www.ingramcontent.com/pod-product-compliance
Lightning Source LLC
Chambersburg PA
CBHW031229250726
48655CB00005B/1877